CONVERSATIONS IN CABS

James McClelland was born in Melbourne in 1915 and studied at Melbourne and Sydney Universities. As both participant and spectator of one of the most interesting periods in Australia's history, he survived a brief political career as a minister in the Whitlam government to become the first chief judge of the Land and Environment Court of NSW in 1980, and in 1984, commissioner for the Royal Commission into British Nuclear Tests at Maralinga.

He describes himself as 'a child of the Great Depression and a fugitive from religion and Marxism . . . a former lawyer without illusions about lawyers; a former judge without illusions about the judiciary and a present journalist without illusions about the media'.

He now writes for the *Sydney Morning Herald* and lives in the Blue Mountains with his third wife, Gillian Appleton.

Also by James McClelland

Stirring the Possum
An Angel Bit the Bride

CONVERSATIONS IN CABS

James McClelland

PENGUIN BOOKS

Penguin Books Australia Ltd
487 Maroondah Highway, PO Box 257
Ringwood, Victoria 3134, Australia
Penguin Books Ltd
Harmondsworth, Middlesex, England
Viking Penguin, A Division of Penguin Books USA Inc.
375 Hudson Street, New York, New York 10014, USA
Penguin Books Canada Limited
10 Alcorn Avenue, Toronto, Ontario, Canada M4V 1E4
Penguin Books (N.Z.) Ltd
182-190 Wairau Road, Auckland 10, New Zealand

First published by Penguin Books Australia, 1991
10 9 8 7 6 5 4 3 2 1

Typeset in Berkley Old Style by Midland Typesetters, Maryborough, Vic.
Made and printed in Australia by The Book Printer

National Library of Australia
Cataloguing-in-Publication data:
McClelland, J. R. (James Robert), 1915-
Conversations in cabs.
ISBN 0 14 014503 6.
1. Australia - Social conditions - 1976-1990. 2. Australia - Social life and customs - 1976-1990. 3. Australia - Politics and government - 1976-1990. 4. Australia - social conditions - 1990- . 5. Australia - Social life and customs - 1990- . 6. Australia - Politics and government - 1990- . I. Title. II. Title: Sydney morning herald.
994.06

NOTE
The article entitled 'Clyde's Comrades' was first published in the *Independent Monthly* and all other pieces first appeared in the *Sydney Morning Herald*. The date of first publication is included at the end of each article. The author and publishers gratefully acknowledge the help of both papers.

For my wife, Gillian ('the Bride' of these pieces), who suggested some and improved all of them.

CONTENTS

FOREWORD	ix
OUR TOLERANCE OF INTOLERANCE	1
BLACK DEATHS REPORT NEEDS WILLPOWER	4
EGO 1 *v* EGO 2 – SO WHAT?	7
CONVERSATIONS IN CABS	10
LITTLE PEACE FOR THOSE WHO SEEK IT	12
SOMEONE'S AFTER YOUR JOB, SISTERS	15
FRED'S ANGELS MEET THE GAYS – AND A GOOD TIME IS HAD BY ALL	18
MARXISM IS AS DEAD AS A DODO	21
MILITANT GREYS? JUST PASS THE RED	24
ANOTHER 'FAMOUS' DAY TO RECALL – AND AN UNHISTORICAL CABBIE	26
ONE IN THE EYE FOR THE HORSEY SET	29
RUSH FOR A QUICK FIX	32
TOMORROW'S POLLIES NEED YESTERDAY'S INSPIRATION	35
A TIMELY REMINDER	38
THE FOUL PART OF POLITICS	41
THAT OLD FAMILIAR FEELING	43
A PLEASANT STROLL IN A CEMETERY	46
IRONING IN THE SOUL	49
THE BURGLAR WASN'T ALL BAD	51
WHO SAYS INDEPENDENT IS A DIRTY WORD?	54
CLYDE'S COMRADES	57
NOVEMBER 11? WHAT HAPPENED?	62
LABOR, THE PARTY THAT IS NO MORE	65
FUN? HEY, WE COULD TAX THAT	68
BENEFITS THAT AGE, ALONE, CANNOT WITHER	71
HOW SYDNEY CAN STILL BE SAVED	73
PRECIOUS CITY OF THE SOUTH	76

ART SUBSIDIES HIGHLIGHT THE THEATRE OF THE ABSURD 79
MOUNTAINS OF THE MOONSTRUCK 82
TIME TO KILL OFF THE DEATH PENALTY 85
FEDERATION DAY, YES, BUT NOT IN THIS MORONIC MONTH 88
BIG BROTHER IS WATCHING, AND WAITING 91
CAPITALISTS CANNOT AFFORD TO CROW 94
DOUBTS STILL LINGER OVER BUTHELEZI 98
BUSH AND HISTORY'S HARSH FOLLY 101
THE KURDS HAVE TV ON THEIR SIDE 104
IS THE TOUGH GUY IMAGE WORTH IT? 107
YABSLEYISM VIEWED FROM THE INSIDE 110
THE VIEW IS DIFFERENT FROM A HOSPITAL BED 112
THE EERIE SOUNDS OF SILENCE 115
DOWN IN THE DUMPS ABOUT SLACK RECYCLING 118
NOBODY CAN BE AN ISLAND THESE DAYS 121
JUSTICE BY JURY SYSTEM THREATENED 124
SIREN CALL OF ADELAIDE STIRS AN OLD MAN 127
IF THINGS AIN'T WHAT THEY USED TO BE, THANK YOUR LUCKY STARS 130
ABORIGINAL IMAGES IN PERSPECTIVE 133
CAUTION, BIG OBJECTS ON THE ROAD 135
CHARMED LIVES, ALL NINE OF THEM 138
A GERIATRIC SACRIFICE TO THE ELECTRONIC AGE 141
POLITICAL FOOTBALL AND THE POPULARITY STAKES 144
SENTENCING POLICY AND LIFETIMES OF REGRET 147
THE STING IS WORSE THAN THE BARK 149
COME AND SEE US SOME (OTHER) TIME 152
I LOVE MUM AND MOZART 155
WHY JAMES INSTEAD OF JASON? 157
BAH, HUMBUG TO THIS SILLY FEEDING FRENZY 159
DULL CHORES OF THE RICH AND FAMOUS 162
A REPUBLIC? AXE THE STATES FIRST 165
FATHOMING THE MAGIC OF A GENIUS 168
WHITE: MOVING, PROFOUND AND DUTIFUL 171
EVERY HOST DESERVES A ROMEO 173

FOREWORD

This collection of my weekly columns in the *Sydney Morning Herald* (plus one article which appeared in the *Independent Monthly*) contains only a couple of pieces that deal with conversations with cabbies. Nevertheless, the title is justified by the contributions that these purveyors of truth, falsehood and scuttlebutt have made over the years to my nodding acquaintance with what is going on in the world.

Reality is hard to hold on to, especially for politicians and judges - and I have been both. When I was a member of federal parliament I would return from my sojourns in Canberra and give my wife my version of the week's events in the nation's capital. I was often surprised to discover that the matters of great pith and moment in which I had partaken were often quite differently interpreted by those, like my wife, who lived in the real world. Similarly, the gravitas that judges don with their medieval robes of office sometimes tends to immure them from salutary contact with ordinary mortals.

The title of this book may be regarded as a metaphor for keeping one's feet on the ground.

OUR TOLERANCE OF INTOLERANCE

Are we a tolerant people? If we accept the definition of the *Shorter Oxford English Dictionary*, a person who can be so described is 'one who tolerates opinions or practices different from his own'.

I never quarrel with that authority, but since tolerant is a word of approval, surely that definition requires some refinement? Is it estimable to be tolerant of Nazism, or wife-beating, or political corruption? I would prefer to categorise such attitudes as moral indifference or even callousness. Tolerance of *all* opinions or practices is an abnegation of ethical standards.

Almost everybody has one or more pet intolerances. In the case of born-again anti-nicotinists like my wife, it is likely to be smokers. When they are around, she flails the air, as though pursuing a horde of flies or mosquitoes. But she's not in favour of sending smokers to jail. I would call hers a tolerant intolerance.

More insidious is unacknowledged intolerance, like that of those who bar Jews or blacks from their clubs while indignantly denying they are anti-Semitic or anti-colour. They would absolve themselves from such a charge by saying something like 'they wouldn't feel comfortable here, we need people who fit in'.

Such attitudes, although in a much less virulent form, are more common than we may suppose. Let's take a look at the question of religious intolerance.

The abatement in sectarianism which has happened during my lifetime is, in my view, to be attributed not primarily to increased religious tolerance but to pervasive indifference to religion itself. If you don't believe in or don't care about

God, what difference does it make whether someone is Catholic or Protestant?

But there are religions besides Christianity, with its decreasingly antagonistic sects. In the past we weren't concerned about them because there were so few of their practitioners around. But the increasing mobility of people of different races and customs which is characteristic of our era has changed all that. Are Australians tolerant, for instance, of Muslims? The answer is: probably not.

Here is an example. In 1987, an application came before the Bankstown local council for the establishment of a Muslim school. The council, obviously bowing to public pressure, turned down the application. The opponents of the proposal denied any suggestion of religious prejudice, but used excuses like increased traffic problems to justify their opposition. Such considerations did not trouble them where other schools and churches in the area were concerned. The Muslims took the matter to the Land and Environment Court and an enlightened judge upheld their appeal.

Last year, the Buddhists were on the receiving end of religious intolerance. A group of them approached the Strathfield council for permission to build a temple in Homebush. All sorts of objections surfaced in the local community, although no objectors mentioned their aversion to saffron robes. Once again, the council, as the interpreter of local opinion, knocked back the proposal. Once again, the Land and Environment Court came down on the side of tolerance, and allowed the Buddhists' appeal.

Then there is the form of intolerance sanctified by the imprimatur of the intelligentsia. In a recent (February 10) issue of the English weekly the *Spectator*, there is a revealing piece by a lapsed Muslim in which he related an incident at a party where a woman journalist told a Muslim friend of his: 'I'm not talking to you any more because of the way Muslims treat women.'

He goes on to complain that the persecution of Salman Rushdie by fundamentalist Muslims (which he deplores) seems to have conferred on people who would consider themselves enlightened the right to abuse all Muslims. They make absurd generalisations 'in a way which, if the word "Jew" or "black" was used, would instantly and obviously be seen to be both nonsensical and distasteful'.

He points out that there are one billion Muslims or people of Muslim birth around the world, of dozens of races and cultures. Muslims, he says, have as broad a spectrum of attitudes to their religion as you might find among Christians or Jews. These range from lapsed, through liberal, to devout, to fundamentalist.

The arguments of those members of the intelligentsia who label all Muslims as fundamentalists 'often rely on a literal reading of the Koran which the great majority of people called Muslims wouldn't go along with, just as the great majority of Christians don't go along with a literal reading of the Bible'.

And so, Muslims get labelled a mob of 'book-burning wife-beaters'. Let our own sometimes self-righteous intelligentsia take note.

To me, the most obscene form of intolerance is that which cloaks itself in the garb of moral superiority, usually in God's name. The paradigm is Fred Nile. His obsession with matters of sexual morality, as interpreted by himself, has conferred on him the right to interpret (his) God's will more infallibly – and intolerantly – than any pope. When he prayed for rain to ruin the Gay and Lesbian Mardi Gras, and it duly rained, he was confirmed in his certainty of having a direct line to his God. As gay activist Lex Watson wittily pointed out in a letter to this paper, God must also dislike opera – it also rained on Opera in the Park.

If I were a praying man, I would be on my knees beseeching God to let Fred know, via their direct line, that it is He, Fred's all-knowing, all-powerful God, who makes people gay or lesbian and that, if Fred were to discover that his own preference were homosexual, God wouldn't mind in the least if he came out of the closet. I'd rather like to see Fred in drag up on one of those floats in Oxford Street on the big night.

I have sworn off politics for the duration of the Federal election (perhaps even for ever) but I can't do justice to a column on intolerance without remarking on its near disappearance between practising politicians in this country.

How can you expect Tweedledum to hate Tweedledee?

1 March 1990

BLACK DEATHS REPORT NEEDS WILLPOWER

What is the purpose of a royal commission? I was recently asked to provide a facetious reply to that question for inclusion in the program for *The Royal Commission into the Australian Economy*, a satirical show which had a successful season at Sydney's Belvoir Street Theatre.

I replied to the effect that it was a device employed by governments to sweep under the rug a problem which they either could not or did not want to solve. There is some, though by no means the whole, truth in that sportive definition.

Whatever reasons motivated the setting up of the royal commissions of recent years, a great deal turned out to be unsweepable. As a result, fact has again provided even more entertainment than fiction. Just think of the Fitzgerald Inquiry, which brought so many Queensland notables undone, and the WA Inc commission, undoubtedly the most revealing striptease show running anywhere in Australia.

But one royal commission of recent years comes close to fitting my ironical definition: the Maralinga commission, over which I presided. The fate of its report provides a warning of what must not be allowed to happen to the recently published report of the Royal Commission into Black Deaths in Custody.

That report indicts us all: for active or passive racism, or the less serious but still grievous charge of moral indifference; for a pervasive police culture of which lying and brutality are normal ingredients; for cynical official cover-ups; for governmental neglect, inaction and hypocrisy.

My experience in the Maralinga inquiry, which also (though not exclusively) included questions affecting Aboriginal people, makes me highly sceptical that any real remedial action will result from the latest commission's report.

The Royal Commission into British Nuclear Tests in Australia during the 1950s, which has come to be known as the Maralinga commission, was set up on 16 July 1984, and its report and recommendations were handed to the Governor General on 20 November 1985.

The pressure for that inquiry had come from (among others) Aboriginal interests complaining about the dangerous condition of the test sites in central Australia.

After we had taken extensive evidence in several cities and towns in Australia, inspected the relevant sites and heard further evidence in London, we reached the following conclusions, which are relevant to the present subject:

That, despite the British claim to have cleaned up the ranges at Maralinga and Emu, where the tests had taken place, and the Holt Government's supine acceptance of that assurance, the Maralinga site was left heavily contaminated with plutonium (which has a half-life of 240 000 years), beryllium and uranium. Further, that there was a significant hazard to Aborigines using the test sites, especially from the plutonium.

The royal commission recommended that action should be commenced *immediately* to clean up the test sites to a level where they would be fit for unrestricted habitation by their traditional Aboriginal occupants as soon as practicable; and that the British – who, after all, had befouled the area lent to them by their admirer Bob Menzies, without consulting even his Cabinet – should pay for the clean-up.

What's the position today, 5½ years after the Federal

Government got our report? The plutonium and other hazardous substances are still there and a start has not yet been made on cleaning up the mess. The intervening time has been consumed by a Technical Assessment Group exploring the best way to clean up the contaminated areas in the light of the estimated cost of the options.

It is true that the commission had recommended the setting up of such an expert body, but we had not imagined it could, even at the most leisurely public service pace, take more than a year or so to complete its task.

That task has at last been completed and the group's report is in the hands of the Government. But now, of course, the Government has a couple of years only in which to consider it before facing the electors. As a consequence, it will probably never get around to doing anything about the problem we were appointed to investigate nearly seven years ago. In the meantime, the Government has survived two elections and if, miraculously, it was to survive another, it could, in the hope that the public had forgotten about it, let it sink quietly in a morass of bureaucratic inaction. My half-joking definition begins to look almost accurate.

By the way, the British are refusing to pay up. Here's Hawke's chance to stand up to a 'great and powerful friend'.

What's the betting?

So don't hold your breath waiting for something to be done about this latest and far more important report. Its disclosures help us to understand how a Labor Government can award the Order of Australia to a trampler on human rights like Turkish President Turgut Ozal. Seeing that our own performance in this field is, as Ozal has cheekily pointed out, not so glorious, why should *his* record disqualify him from our highest honour?

The Royal Commission into Aboriginal Deaths in Custody has come up with hard-headed, practical suggestions for lifting our game in the treatment of our Aboriginal fellow citizens.

If any tangible result is to ensue, a mighty leap in the will of governments and people will be necessary. It would help if the media treated the commission's findings and recommendations as something more than a one-day event.

22 May 1991

EGO 1 *v* EGO 2 – SO WHAT?

Here is a parable of our times.

Last Friday, the long-awaited clash occurred between Ego No 1 and Ego No 2. Media hype had prepared us over a period of a couple of years for what was billed as an earth-shaking event, a battle of titans, a climacteric in our nation's destiny.

Yes, whether Bob Hawke or Paul Keating should lead us out of the economic quagmire in which their policies have landed us.

It seemed to me, and I suspect to a lot of voters, that a more realistic question was: when would both these shop-soiled exhibitionists do the decent thing by getting out and giving some less-tainted member of their tribe like, say, John Kerin, a chance to try to clear up their mess?

So the big day came and, after a great deal of buffoonery, ended in total confusion. The protagonists retreated for the weekend to their lairs, accompanied by their various sages and spear-carriers.

Millions of words were spilled in the next couple of days speculating on what was going on in the thickets of political intrigue to shore up the prospects of the gladiators for Monday's adjourned fight to the death.

My weekend was not spent in a state of panting excitement over a drama, which, the pundits implied, made all else – including the football and the races – matters of minimal concern. On the Saturday night, I had committed myself to speak at a meeting in one of our local hamlets to mark the thirtieth anniversary of Amnesty International.

The 'trivial' subjects which occupied the meeting included what could be done to relieve the plight of hundreds of thousands of people throughout the world who are imprisoned, many subjected to torture, not because of any crime but solely for what they believe in – the 'prisoners of conscience'.

On the Sunday night, I officiated again, this time at a concert organised by Community Aid Abroad to raise money for emergency relief for victims of famine in the Horn of Africa – Eritrea, Tigre and Ethiopia. Drought and the devastation of a 30-year war, now mercifully nearing an end, have placed at least two million people in imminent danger of death from starvation.

The star of the concert was the talented singer Margret Roadknight, who is ever willing to aid a good cause. Less famous no doubt than the two gladiators in Canberra but, as it struck me at the time, perhaps doing a more useful – and certainly more entertaining – job.

Ever since my brief career in politics ended some years ago, I have marvelled at the awesome lack of perspective of that trade.

Their extravagant view of their own importance, measured against the immensity of human travail, is, of course, fanned by journalists who become infected by the same disease.

How many parliamentarians, I wonder, took time out to ask themselves: what is this Homeric contest all about? What great principle is at stake? As usual, Keating had a pithy answer: 'I wanted his job and tried to take it off him. It's as simple as that.'

As to the pious indignation about Hawke's lying to the electorate about his intention, in the light of his pact with Keating, to see out his term as leader after the 1990 election, the Keating camp blithely ignores the fact that it takes at least two to make a conspiracy and that Keating was in it up to his neck.

I do not see any sign that public indignation at Hawke's

duplicity is as great as some are portraying it to be. A cynical Australian public has long been inured to this kind of behaviour on the part of politicians, and many people probably suspected all along that there had been some kind of deal. John Button once as good as said so publicly.

And how many people did Keating think he was fooling when he proclaimed after the ballot: 'As far as I'm concerned there will be no second challenge'? After all, we have lost count of the number of times he denied he was going to throw his hat into the ring, while his thuggish NSW right-wing acolytes touted vigorously for him behind the scenes. As he sat with hooded eyes on the back bench, he looked every inch the assassin in waiting.

Even more astonishing to me was the fact that any Labor member should imagine that the party's chances of re-election would be improved by appointing the erstwhile Treasurer as their leader. If they took time to talk occasionally to those who decide their fate, they would learn how widespread Keating's unpopularity is.

I freely confess that I was once dazzled by him and thought he should be leader. But the scales fell from my eyes, and I came to regard him as a snake-oil salesman.

What the politicians evidently overlook is that ordinary Australians, especially those who have either lost, or fear losing, their jobs, and the many thousands who are having trouble meeting their mortgage payments, are less than enthralled by the vaudeville show in which Keating has been the star performer.

People blame their tribulations on the man who promised them a soft landing and then gave them the recession they had to have. And they will not forgive him.

5 June 1991

Conversations in Cabs

Politicians who are interested in finding out what's happening in the real world could do worse than shed the big white Commonwealth car occasionally and catch a cab.

Cab drivers, some of whom are taciturn and some garrulous, are uniquely placed to pick up the scuttlebutt, the wisdom, the folly of human discourse. They are one-man polling organisations.

Of course, riding in cabs is a bit of a lottery. You may be unlucky enough to score a soap-shy chain-smoker with his radio at full blast, spewing out the profundities of one of the Far-Right talkers-back who abound on the airwaves these days.

But one of the bonuses of the Keating-led recession, at least for cab-users, is that some pretty smart people find themselves today, due to the lack of jobs appropriate to their talents and training, behind the wheel of a cab.

During the recent period of more-than-normal political turbulence (both Federal and State), I have ridden in a few cabs. The air was thick with the lucubrations of political pundits, but I found the throwaway comments of cabbies at least as enlightening.

One wanted to know why a clever fellow like Paul Keating thought it would be any harder for Bob Hawke to break a promise just because there were witnesses to it. Another, commenting while the result of the NSW election hung in the balance, said that, judging by the remarks of his customers, he could have told the Libs they had never had it in the bag. 'Hungarians are usually pretty smart,' he opined. 'That Greiner must be the only one of them who's a mug. You'd never catch Peter Abeles in trouble.' (This cabbie obviously does not read the financial press.)

I should interpolate here that on my occasional forays into the city, my preferred form of transport is by State Government bus. I take a taxi only when I'm in a hurry. Sadly, I have to report that this doesn't always work. Those who 'plan' our cities have succeeded in making it so hard to find your way about that even those whose job it is to know the best way to get from A to B are performing increasingly like bushies.

Just the other day a cabbie I engaged to take me to the Darling Harbour Convention Centre ended up at the Ultimo Fish Markets and professed himself totally bemused about where to go from there. I eventually got to my destination 10 minutes late, thus cancelling out the rationale for taking a cab in the first place.

Whenever I have taken a cab in London I have marvelled at the nonchalant ease with which the cab drivers, without ever asking for further particulars, infallibly delivered me to my destination, even when the journey seemed to be labyrinthine.

It is certainly no easier to find your way about London than Sydney. But to get a cab driver's licence there it is necessary to pass a most difficult exam known in the trade as The Knowledge. I'm told it's almost as hard as getting into the Melbourne Club. If finding your way about Sydney becomes any more difficult, it will be necessary, not only for cabbies, but for all drivers to pass a similar test.

So don't blame your cabbie if he loses his way in this motorist's nightmare. Nearly every time we visit the place we are reminded of one of the most potent reasons for living elsewhere. Without ever facing up to the root cause of clogged streets and increased pollution, the authorities are constantly creating further difficulties for motorists. The result is that drivers are regularly being confronted with the Roads and Traffic Authority's 'Changed Traffic Conditions'.

This may have almost suicidal consequences. One day last week, the Bride dropped me in George Street to perform a brief errand. There was no hope of parking anywhere nearby so she drove off, blithely calling: 'I'll drive around the block and pick you up here.'

Half an hour later the woman who arrived to pick me up was unrecognisable from the amiable one who had dropped me. After encountering half a dozen 'no left (or no right) turns', two or three 'no entries' or 'cabs and buses only' signs, she was close to hysteria. She had finally managed to get back to me only by taking an illegal left and navigating a 'cabs and buses only,' section of Market Street. If prosecuted, she intends to plead not guilty because of temporarily unsound mind due to governmental harassment.

On reflection, I suppose the authorities are to be applauded for making it harder for private car drivers to find their way about in the city. To the periodic bucolic visitor, if not to those benumbed into acceptance of the quotidian agony, it is blindingly obvious that the only solution to the problem of traffic congestion is to ban from the city all vehicles except buses, service vehicles and cabs.

Instead, our 'planners' encourage the construction of more and more parking spaces in the CBD, while the grotesquely expensive harbour tunnel will bring more cars into town. Why do people leave Sydney?

12 June 1991

LITTLE PEACE FOR THOSE WHO SEEK IT

Having been around for a few wars and taken part in one, I have detected a common factor in all of them – the denigration, mounting in frenzy as things go badly, of all who question the wisdom of our embroilment. The Gulf War is no exception.

I was touched by a letter published in this paper last Friday in which an opponent of the war spoke of the ridicule and contempt poured on 'peaceniks' in the print and electronic media, and entered a plea: 'Let us argue our cases with passion and not rancour, with logic and not bile, in peace and not anger'.

Hear, hear! But I hold out little hope that his plea will be heard. Coincidentally, on the day before that letter was published, I received from a reader of this column a copy of a piece which had caught his eye, headed: 'Why the Peace Movement is a "Rabble of Misfits" '.

It had appeared recently in the Coffs Harbour *Advocate* and was written by Lauchlan Chipman, who is described as philosophy professor at Wollongong University. Those questioning the wisdom of Australia's participation in the Gulf War are dubbed 'the indecent minority'. Chipman heaps scorn on the signatories of an anti-war advertisement which appeared in metropolitan dailies shortly before our troops were committed to action, especially on 'the usual suspects'. This list includes Manning Clark, Tom Keneally, Tom Uren, Dr Helen Caldicott and Sir Ronald Wilson.

He reserves his strongest venom for the last-named, despite or more likely because he enjoys considerable esteem in the community as a former justice of the High Court of Australia, present chairman of the Federal Human Rights and Equal Opportunities Commission and president of the National Assembly of the Uniting Church in Australia. He is also one of the royal commissioners into WA Inc – a record, I would have thought, which should ensure that his views are taken seriously.

The peace movement as a whole is branded as a 'rabble of layabouts, malcontents, sexual misfits, anti-Semites, PLO apologists, American-haters, vegetarians and other "concerned citizens" '. (Poor old vegetarians!)

The denigration of a cause by gutter abuse of its adherents becomes more difficult when the conduct of a war by your own side falters. Inevitably, more and more people whom it is difficult to brand as knaves or dupes or fools come out against it, as they did in the Vietnam War.

The net of vituperation then has to be cast more widely and people of impeccable repute have to be added to the list. Chipman will now have to add to his list the name of an internationally renowned scholar of strategic studies who is regularly consulted by the Department of Defence and a number of foreign governments.

I refer to Professor Des Ball, the head of the Strategic and Defence Studies Centre at the Australian National University. He is reported, in last Friday's *Sydney Morning Herald*, commenting on our participation in the war: 'On balance, it is probably not in our national interest to be involved.'

He stated that our primary strategic interests were in our own region and that these might actually be damaged by our participation in the Gulf War, especially in view of the Government's failure to consult these countries before making such a commitment. While conceding our interest in a more stable Middle East, he does not believe this war will achieve it. 'The antagonisms created by the war will last for many years after the Americans win this battle,' Ball concludes.

And surely Pope John Paul II must qualify for Chipman's list. The pontiff is reported in the *Catholic Weekly* of 16 January as saying: 'A peace obtained through arms, which left intact the deep causes of violence in this part of the world, could only lay the groundwork for new violence.'

The world's self-appointed policeman, the US, will not be able to impose a Pax Americana on the Middle East. Its mandate from the UN for the use of force was limited to the removal of Iraqi forces from Kuwait. Despite the escalation of this objective by the more gung ho of America's leaders into a program of destroying Saddam and his entire war machine, it becomes clearer every day that this is not on.

The Soviet Union, without whose support the UN's seal of approval could be withdrawn, has made it clear it will not be a party to the destruction of Iraq. Last week's joint US-Soviet offer of a ceasefire in return for an Iraqi undertaking to withdraw from Kuwait makes it clear that the US has been forced to retreat to the limited objective. After oceans of blood, as well as rivers of oil, have been spilt, Saddam will probably still be there.

The Prime Minister's bullying of the ABC to report the war as a straightforward contest of good versus evil cannot conceal the fact that he has led us into a war in which there can be no winners.

6 February 1991

SOMEONE'S AFTER YOUR JOB, SISTERS

Unemployment is engraved on the heart of any child of the Great Depression, of whom I am one. More than 30 per cent were out of work when I arrived on the labour market in the 1930s and as I watch the figures creep up today I wonder if we are going to have to call this recession by a grimmer name.

In those days, since no solution was forthcoming from the economists whose ignorance of their own system, much like today, had produced the disaster, it was not surprising that there was a profusion of magical cures.

One such cure was Social Credit, invented by a certain Major Douglas. His nostrum was for the Government to abolish taxation and also to make periodic monetary gifts to its citizens to make up for the inadequacy of purchasing power. So far this time around we've had nothing quite as wild as that.

But a commentator who must be taken seriously, Mr B. A. Santamaria, has come up with an answer comparable in its alluring simplicity to that of Major Douglas. His prescription for unemployment is: get as many married women as possible out of the workforce and back where they belong, in the home. Jobs will then become available for 'male breadwinners who wish to fulfil the purpose for which God, or nature, has assigned them'.

Mr Santamaria asserts (the *Weekend Australian*, May 4-5): 'The central – although not the only – reason for the displacement of adult male breadwinners and for the reduction in teenage job opportunities is the large-scale absorption of married women into the workforce, particularly into part-time work. More than 50 per cent of married women are now in the paid workforce, compared with some 20 per cent in 1960.'

He does not go so far as to assert that there is any direct causal relationship between the percentage of women in paid employment and the phenomenon of recurring economic downturns in a capitalist society. The facts are against such a claim. A far lower female percentage than today in the workforce did not prevent or mitigate the onset of the Great Depression.

On Mr Santamaria's own admission, the percentage of married women in today's paid workforce is 'almost uniform throughout the Western world'. But underlining the irrelevance of that factor to a country's economic performance, some of them (members of the European Community, as well as Japan) are in glowing health compared with sickly Australia. Obviously, we must look elsewhere for the cause of debility.

None of these facts disturbs Mr Santamaria's conviction that our present balance of men and married women in the workforce is against the natural order and must be corrected.

He is careful to exclude sanctions against the employment of married women: 'no legal obstacle should be placed in the way of a woman entering the workforce if she so wishes'.

But since it is his view that most married women who seek paid work do so solely from economic compulsion, he proposes a course of legislative action providing a disincentive for them to do so.

He suggests that payroll tax be taken back from the States and resumed by the Commonwealth, and that it be used exclusively for the payment of family allowances (per child), plus a homemaker's allowance, to be paid to all married women who choose not to enter the workforce. Such governmental action will, he asserts without adducing any evidence, have the result that 'some 60 per cent of married women will soon drop out of the workforce'.

Without considering the philosophical underpinnings of this program, one or two practical problems emerge. The political difficulties of making the tax switch he proposes are not trivial. And then, a fairly substantial increase in the amount of money raised by means of payroll tax would be required to ensure that no drop in the standard of living was involved for families changing from two-income to one-income support. Otherwise, surely the anticipated 60 per cent dropout of married women might turn out to be wildly over-optimistic. I hope Mr Santamaria's sums also take account of the fact that, as more and more employers go broke, the payroll tax pool, instead of expanding, dries up.

I would also need some pretty solid evidence, based on careful research, to be convinced that 60 per cent of employed married women would prefer to be at home than at work, provided they were no worse off financially. Mr Santamaria takes a passing swipe at feminists who go to work for 'fulfilment' (his inverted commas imply that's silly or perhaps even sinful), and I suspect that Simone de Beauvoir, Germaine Greer, Betty Friedan and their ilk loom large among the devils he holds accountable for today's social ills.

The time has long passed when it was considered appropriate for men to pontificate about what is good for women and to advocate measures designed to satisfy God's or nature's alleged intentions for them.

Implicit in Mr Santamaria's nostrum is the suggestion that women are unqualified to make decisions for themselves – are, in fact, inherently inferior to men. At a time of crisis like today, I fear the superficial appeal, especially to unreconstructed males, of social solutions aimed at extruding women from the workforce.

In recent articles Mr Santamaria has been an eloquent

debunker of the economic rationalists who have got us into our present mess. In this case, however, I fear that dogma has led him as far astray as it has led them.

15 May 1991

FRED'S ANGELS MEET THE GAYS – AND A GOOD TIME IS HAD BY ALL

'What has been the Soviet Union's approach to the question of homosexuality?' I once asked a devout Australian Stalinist. 'We've abolished it,' he replied.

This was in the era of total and unquestioning acceptance by local communists of the entire Russian catechism, long before Gorbachev, perestroika or glasnost were even dreamed of.

The thought struck me then, and has stayed with me ever since, that the notion that anything should be 'done' about homosexuality is essentially totalitarian.

It is not surprising that Hitler and Stalin should have regarded it as something to be eradicated. The essence of totalitarian regimes is conformism and this involves unbending intolerance of any beliefs or practises regarded as deviant.

To Nazi or Marxist dictators, being gay was as unacceptable as being a Jew, a gypsy or a democrat because it stood in the way of complete possession by the State of your mind and your soul.

As I have written before, the fatal flaw of Marxism was a naive overestimation of the possibility of altering the nature of men and women.

When my wife and I visited China as tourists in 1978, we were told the same thing: there were no gays any more in China. Our eyes told us otherwise. Strolling along the banks of the Whampoa River in Shanghai one night when we had shed our ever-present official guide, we were struck by the frequency of fondling couples of the same sex.

It is more surprising that people should declare war on homosexuality in the name of Christ. It was with these thoughts in mind that I attended last Monday's Solemn Assembly of Repentance and Intercession in Taylor Square, conducted by Fred Nile as part of his crusade against the annual Gay Mardi Gras - and sexual deviance generally.

As was to be expected, the gay community was out in force. If Ian Paisley were to organise an anti-Catholic demo in St Peter's Square, you would expect a few Catholics to show up to let him know their eradication would be no walkover. To Sydney gays, Taylor Square is their St Peter's.

Thanks to good organisation on both sides, it was a pretty good show. The gays and lesbians were there a couple of hours earlier than Fred's angels, good humouredly mocking the small band of black revivalist singers on the platform set up outside the gates of the imposing old criminal court building in readiness for Fred's sermon from the mount.

There were gay placards in abundance including one which proclaimed 'Repent, Relent, Redecorate' and another which reminded the gathering that Christ liked whores and knocked around with 12 single men.

At one stage, while waiting for Fred's arrival, the gays were shepherded by one of their marshals around into Forbes Street where they held a religious service of their own conducted by a clergyman wearing a silver cross, who made out what sounded to me like a pretty good case that there was no necessary incompatibility between being Christian and being gay.

Taylor Square has a certain raffishness which seemed appropriate to the occasion. The fronds of the recently planted palms on Gilligan's Island (a little vacant triangle at the junction of its intersecting streets) waved in the sharp breeze and the usual crop of derros sipping their fiery brews in the doorways of the old shops seemed to have vacated the scene for the day. It occurred to me that Fred might have arranged a private sweet sherry beano for them so that they would not add their mite of sin to the Square.

There was an air of carnival rather than of religious fervour. There was some, but not much, sipping of stubbies and cans.

Finally Fred and his flock arrived. Most of them seemed to be from out of town. His organisation had evidently bussed their adherents from country centres. The provincials, carrying banners indicating their provenance, seemed greatly to outnumber the urban zealots, giving the procession an overwhelmingly bumpkin flavour.

I don't know much about the social composition of Fred's sect but an impressionistic assessment could be drawn from the appearance of those following his banner on Monday that his real demographic base is the provincial poor.

As they journeyed through the streets of Sodom, some of them, especially the young children, looked scared; some displayed moral nausea and others looked just plain bewildered. Some waved Bibles at the sinners, some chanted prayers, others sang hymns. An efficient, well-drilled array of police, including a few on splendidly behaved horses, separated the pure from the sullied.

My strongest impression was of the irrationality and futility of it all. Fred's flock might as sensibly have been engaged in a crusade against the left-handed or the blue-eyed. I wondered if it occurred to any of them that Fred Nile's God might have something to do with all these human conditions. If, as they believe, we are all God's creatures, why should we need His forgiveness for being what He made us?

I found Fred's answer to this sort of heretical thinking in the roneoed Order-of-the Day he had issued to his troops setting out the procedures of the rally. The program for Taylor Square included the following:

'Leader: In the name of Jesus and in His wounds is the victory. We proclaim His victory over the works of the devil, over all the pornography and obscenity that is flooding our land through films, videos, literature and the homosexual Mardi Gras.

'All: Jesus is victor. He has come to destroy the works of the devil.'

So there you have it. There is a division of functions between the two supernatural powers. It may be God who makes you left-handed or blue-eyed. But it is the devil who makes you gay.

In any event, a good time was had by all.

5 October 1989

MARXISM IS AS DEAD AS A DODO

Recently, I received a letter from a man of my own generation who had at various times occupied some of the highest positions in the Communist Party of Australia, which is now, for all practical purposes, defunct. He asked me whether I would read and comment on his just-completed manuscript of recollections of his life as a communist.

Although I have never met him, his name is a household word in leftist circles. I readily agreed to his request, while reflecting wryly on the twists of history. Some forty years ago, after a few years as a card-carrying member of a romantic Marxist group (of the Trotskyist, not the Stalinist communion), I renounced the Marxist religion for ever.

I found the manuscript surprisingly moving, as well as highly informative. When it finds a publisher, as I'm sure it will, this book will be an important contribution to the history of Marxism in this country. Leftism, in the sense of strongly felt dissent from the prevailing social and economic orthodoxies will, I suspect, always be with us. But, as the manuscript makes clear, Marxism as a philosophical and economic doctrine – complete with its own catechism, rosary beads and prayer books – has no future here except on the ratbag fringes of dissent.

Last year the CPA announced that it would shut up shop and would sponsor a new loose leftist congregation not based on Marxism–Leninism. So the few remaining Marxist daily communicants will have no 'church' to go to. This may be an appropriate time for some scholar to sit down and write the definitive history of Marxism in Australia, complete with sects and heresies and gyrations and personalities.

A prominent ex-communist who had been a member of the inner circle has estimated that, at one time or another, somewhere between 100 000 and 200 000 people must have passed through the ranks of the Communist Party. At its highest point of influence, when it seemed that the Red Army was the world's greatest hope of damming the Nazi tide, it was almost a popular party here. A well-known fellow traveller of the CPA, Mrs Jessie Street, came close to winning the silvertail eastern suburbs seat of Wentworth at that time.

But for most of its life the party has been reviled by the vast majority of the population. It was regarded as consisting of fanatics, dupes of the Soviet Union, thugs, union ballot riggers, power maniacs - the whole panoply of political undesirables. And so it did. But, as this manuscript makes clear, it also attracted a large number of idealistic, self-sacrificing people, including the author of the manuscript.

It has always been easy to scoff at the communists, and I have been among the scoffers. Even when Khrushchev blew the whistle on Stalin at the 20th congress in his famous 'secret speech' in 1956, most of the faithful refused to believe that benign old Uncle Joe could have been a bloodstained member of the choice little club of monsters which included Hitler and Genghis Khan. They had swallowed Stalin's alliance with Hitler in 1939, the Moscow trials of 1936-38, the evidence of the gulag provided by, among others, Solzhenitsyn, the Soviet invasions of Hungary in 1956 and Czechoslovakia in 1968, though each of the events had produced schisms and defections.

But surely the adherents of the other great religions have demonstrated a comparable blindness and credulity. They have closed their eyes to the crimes of the popes, the absurdities of creationism, frauds like the Shroud of Turin and the heinous crimes committed in the name of Islam and Christianity.

The appeal of Marxism and the fidelity of its adherents can be explained, despite its claims to scientific rationality, only by treating it as a religion based on a set of unverifiable and, by now, exploded myths. That is what makes the manuscript such a moving document. It is a story of one man's gradual loss of faith as the myths dissolved under the white heat of reality and the scales finally fell from his eyes. The two pillars of Marxist faith that have crumbled for all but the purblind are these:

First, that the practical lessons that life under capitalism teaches the 'working class' (itself hard to define) imbue that class with a consciousness of the necessity of socialism, thus making the working class the motor of social change. But, as the author of the manuscript asks: 'How are we to explain a social scene and politics so widely different from what such propositions would lead us to expect?' Some hard questions arise when decades pass and reality gets further and further away from such a view of what should happen.

Second, that the abolition of the private ownership of the means of production and its replacement by public ownership will abolish inefficiency, exploitation, boom and bust and usher in an era of plenty and a just distribution of the products of labour. It is the comprehensive demolition of this myth, as demonstrated by the exposure of scarcities and corruption in the so-called socialist countries, which has administered the *coup de grâce* to Marxist faith in the countries outside that orbit. Even those within that orbit that still pay lip service to the Marxist religion no longer practise it.

True believers have always dismissed criticism emanating from the tainted source of defenders of capitalism. But capitalism, though in need of major surgery, is still breathing. Marxism is as dead as the dodo.

11 June 1990

MILITANT GREYS? JUST PASS THE RED

Well, it's about time my lot got a bit of recognition! That was my reaction on reading that the Church of England in Britain had just published a paperback called *Ageing*, a 150-page report which has been in gestation for two years.

It is the product of a working party consisting of a professor of community medicine, a professor of social gerontology and a gaggle of clerics.

The message it proclaims is the necessity to combat ageism as ruthlessly as sexism and racism. I agree, but I hope that it does not stir my coevals into hyperactivity and lead to the setting up of a pressure group such as the Grey Panthers in the United States, who proudly declare that they are Glad to be Grey. (Shades of Women Who Want to be Women.) I shudder at the thought of a militant grey movement.

The fact that there are more and more of us is no reason for us elderly to start throwing our weight around. The very fact that our numbers are growing and that age does not disqualify us from voting will ensure that the pollies ignore us at their peril.

If they do, a coalition of grey power and green power might one day claim a parliamentary majority, perhaps led by Malcolm Fraser making a comeback in his eighties. (As Bob Menzies would have put it, heaven forfend!)

I have been a victim of ageism, though of a not particularly wounding kind.

It is generally accepted that most people's looks do not improve with age, but each of us likes to think we are waging a reasonable fight against its ravages.

A few years ago – after a gap of some five years – I encountered the artist Clif Pugh (my junior by ten years) at a convivial lunch. When we were well into the red (bibulously, not financially, speaking), Clif remarked: 'I always wanted to do a portrait of you for the Archibald, Jim, but I can see I have left it too late.' He paused, threw me a painterly scrutiny and asked: 'What happened to your face?'

The Bride, who was within earshot, interjected with more loyalty than tact: 'I think Jim looks ten years younger than you, Clif.'

Well, Clif has now put his cue in the rack, but I'm sure he would not have held it against me that I have proved more durable than him. After all, he didn't leave much in the cup.

A good example of ageism in my own experience is a case I heard during my time on the Land and Environment Court. A local council had rejected a proposal for the development of a retirement village in a salubrious area on the edge of an upmarket suburb. It was at that time rather sparsely populated and the council bowed to the objections of some residents.

Among these was a family which had chosen to live there because the traffic – vehicular and pedestrian – was so light as not to disturb the family members' favoured recreation of riding their horses along the local roads.

They feared that the presence of doddering figures on the roads might frighten the horses and inhibit their own pleasure. On appeal from the council's decision, I allowed the development to proceed. To my way of thinking, the objections exemplified the not-in-my-backyard syndrome: we have nothing against old people but why should we be singled out to put up with them?

A closely related ism is manifested by those who say they have nothing against Muslims but don't want a mosque built in their suburb because it will aggravate traffic congestion.

I'd like to think that concern for the aged and the problems their growing numbers will pose for society will devolve not so much on the old themselves, who have earned a rest from agitation, as on those who are thoughtful enough to recognise that old age will one day overtake them.

There's something a trifle off-putting about the threat of

a new breed of geriatric proselytisers knocking on our doors like Jehovah's Witnesses trying to sell their own brand of salvation.

I won't be ordering the Anglican booklet from my local bookshop. It hardly sounds like my preferred reading. I will assume that its definition of ageism is: discrimination in law, policy or society generally against people purely on the grounds of their age, and I agree that this is something to be strongly resisted.

But the medico-clerical composition of the working party which produced it fills me with foreboding – not about its probable concern with the hereafter and preparing oneself therefore, but about the likelihood of an austere, Jane Fondaesque prescription for eternal life on this earth by dint of self-denial and jogging, the kind of lifestyle achieved by avoiding those very habits which, to me, have always constituted the principal reason for sticking around as long as you can.

24 October 1990

ANOTHER 'FAMOUS' DAY TO RECALL – AND AN UNHISTORICAL CABBIE

For some years the media have cast me in the role of the Dr Springborg of the Kerr War. Just as Springborg has been depicted as a slightly offbeat authority on Iraqi affairs, I have been given a similar place in the unending controversy over the 1975 dismissal of the Whitlam Government by Sir John Kerr.

My somewhat severe criticism of Kerr's action at the time and subsequently would probably not have sufficed to earn me my dubious eminence in this field had it not been for the added ingredient of our long and close friendship before our very public estrangement.

I first heard of Sir John's death in the late afternoon of Monday last week, and was genuinely saddened as at the death of anyone to whom one has once been close. At the same time, I was apprehensive of the likely media onslaught. From past experience, I have the impression that there are lists of potential commentators on any subject in order of preference. On the subject of Sir John Kerr, I seem to run a close second to Gough Whitlam, who on this occasion was maintaining the silence.

I was caught on the hop that day by a Melbourne commercial radio commentator, and Phillip Adams for his Radio National program *Late Night Live.* I also made a recorded comment for the next morning's ABC Radio program, *AM.*

I retired that night fully aware of the perils of the morrow. As luck would have it, I had a longstanding commitment to talk to senior students of a local high school on certain topical matters, namely war and human aggression, and the role of the media in Australia.

Every now and then I succumb to the blandishments of some local teacher, especially if the suggested date is distant enough to seem unlikely ever to arrive. Acceptance is also related to my curiosity about the likelihood of our ever becoming a clever country, since some contact with adolescent thought processes seems relevant to that question. (My experiences so far give grounds for cautious hope.)

The Bride, well aware of the persistence of the media in a feeding frenzy, did not inquire the name of the school, and was under instructions to tell all callers that I was incommunicado until some time in the afternoon. Nothing daunted, the minder of one notoriously aggressive TV pundit threatened to track me down anyway. He did not succeed, but if he had, I wonder if he intended to kidnap me.

Jana Wendt's minders were more suave and diplomatic. If I would agree to be interviewed for *A Current Affair,* the Nine Network would send a helicopter to pick me up and deliver me home, all in a couple of hours. Other callers apparently expected me to drop everything and get to Sydney under my own steam, all for the honour and glory of appearing on their programs.

My first reaction was a flash of insight into why TV companies have got so far into the red. How to justify the expense of sending a helicopter from Willoughby to Katoomba and back merely to extract 10 minutes of comment from an ancient warrior on a battle of long ago?

But if someone chose to be profligate with Kerry Packer's money, who was I to fret? So, at 4 pm a cab arrived to transport me from my house to Melrose Park, Katoomba, a genuine level playing field rather than the metaphorical one so beloved of the deregulationists, which is used as the local helipad.

The cab driver was an easygoing local lad whose interest in historical events and important personages was manifestly slight. But he was in some awe of helicopters. He was clearly wondering what could be so important as to warrant plucking this old codger from his garden and conveying him to Sydney in a chopper.

But his curiosity was aroused. 'Are you famous or something?' he asked. Assuming an appropriately modest look, I launched into a short, simple account of what it was all about. Such was his innocence that I didn't know where to start. 'Have you heard of Sir John Kerr?' I asked. He stared blankly and shook his head. 'Have you heard of Jana Wendt?' His face lit up, 'Yeah,' he responded enthusiastically. 'She's famous.'

I duly went through my paces with the famous Ms Wendt. In the accusatory mode which is apparently required of practitioners of her trade, she did her best to fit me with the blame for the alleged joylessness of Sir John's closing years but, despite her charm and skill, it was difficult to make the charge stick.

3 April 1991

ONE IN THE EYE FOR THE HORSEY SET

A few days ago I received a letter from an outraged citizen. He thought I might be interested to know about a poster advertising a stage production being shown at the Belvoir Street Theatre called *Taboo*.

The letter was signed and carried the writer's address, but I have no way of knowing whether my correspondent is male or female. Nothing really turns on it but, as the writing happens to have a masculine tone I assumed the letter came from a male.

He complained that the poster was pornographic. He had gone to some trouble to expose the object of his wounded moral sensibilities, enclosing two photographs he had taken of the offending poster, from two angles, evidently in case I missed the point.

He had also indulged in considerable research, apparently traipsing the streets of Sydney counting how many posters there were (fifty).

The letter concluded on a rather peremptory note: 'What do you think, Mr McClelland, and more importantly what can you do? I await your reply.'

The first question I asked myself was why I had been singled out as a custodian of public morals. Had anything I have written in this column or elsewhere carried the trademark of the blue-nosed nark? Had my correspondent, perhaps, been put up to it by Fred Nile to test the limits of my permissiveness? Or was it merely because he knew I had been a founding father of the Belvoir Street Theatre and he thought I should accept some responsibility?

He had, in fact, got in touch with Belvoir to register his

protest and to ask that these posters be removed. He had been told that the theatre's management knew nothing about them and accepted no responsibility for the people who put them up. I can believe this; busy theatre people don't have time to go sniffing around the city's walls and the show, though it was staged at Belvoir, was not one of the theatre's own productions. The person to whom he had spoken at the theatre had compounded his sense of outrage by suggesting: 'Sue us, it'll make great publicity for the show.'

But our Savanorola was not so easily silenced. He sought a legal opinion, only to be informed that there was nothing illegal about the poster and resort to the law was not open to him. At this stage I could detect some frothing at the mouth. 'For me, that is a totally unacceptable situation in a society such as ours, based historically on respectful laws and ideals.'

Then came the crunch: 'Also I wonder what to tell my 12-year-old son as we walk past these posters on the street.'

So here is my reply:

Well, Dad, I think you deserve a public answer rather than one for your sensitive eyes and ears alone. As you imply, it is a matter of some public interest.

As far as your 12-year-old son is concerned, as you stroll with him down our Babylonian (to use your own comparison) streets, just don't draw his attention to the poster and it's a 100-to-1 on he won't notice it. Even if he does he'll need your inbuilt sin detector to descry anything wrong with it. I've walked past it in the streets many times and until you pointed out its satanic detail it had escaped my attention. And even if your son does get the message I doubt it will drive him to equophilia. Yours in purity, Jim McClelland.

Sorry, my prurient readers, to have kept you so long in the dark about the specific vice depicted in the poster. Yes, if you look very closely you will espy a puckish fellow with a mischievous grin, short in stature but long in equipment, in a sexual approach to a horse.

The prints sent to me were rather blurred, but I suspect a microscopic scrutiny would disclose another figure exhibiting a rampant phallus to the same distinctly indifferent horse.

The scene is extracted from one of those countless frescoes which adorn ancient buildings, including temples, in places such as India, Indonesia, Cambodia and, I suggest, almost everywhere. This particular example is a part of a famous fresco from one of India's most sacred temples and I imagine the message of the poster is that what is taboo in one culture would not cause a murmur in another.

This particular one is a bit of a giggle; I doubt it can ever have been considered a commercial for the sexual preferability of horses to people.

If, when our sheltered 12-year-old grows up, he elects to travel to ancient centres of civilisation he will have to spend a lot of his time averting his gaze from objects of art if he is to avoid the moral contamination which his parent at present apprehends.

Even in a country like ours, whose citizens notoriously display an excessive interest in horses, I would take some convincing that, in the unlikely event such posters were plastered over the walls of every suburb in our wicked city, they would trigger a stampede by our youth from the bedrooms to the stables.

If you go looking for pornography with a magnifying glass you'll find it almost wherever the glass falls. Porn is in the eye of the beholder.

This is not to say that all pornography is unobjectionable. When it involves young children as objects or combines sex with physical cruelty, it passes the bounds of the socially acceptable and, in so far as it is possible, attempts should be made to prevent its display.

But any alleged social damage which my correspondent attributes to posters such as the one to which he objects is, in my view, so unlikely and so trivial that it does not warrant the attention of the authorities.

3 May 1990

RUSH FOR A QUICK FIX

The Australian Government is on the verge of taking a decision which may set back the cause of drug law reform in this country by twenty years.

Last December, a United Nations convention on illicit drug trafficking adopted an international treaty which extends and reinforces the prohibitionist policy in earlier treaties. Australia, along with sixty-five other countries, was a signatory.

Though there is a growing body of informed opinion that the prohibition and penalisation of the use of hard drugs such as heroin has been a spectacular failure everywhere it has been tried, Australia's signature to the treaty was not preceded by any parliamentary or public debate. Apart from a few officials in Canberra, there would be few people in this country who know of the treaty's existence.

The treaty is, of course, not binding on the citizens of any signatory country until and unless it is ratified by the government of that country. This involves the simple matter of a ratification document being signed by the minister of foreign affairs and being filed at the UN headquarters in New York. It does not even require the approval of parliament.

The only signatory which has ratified the treaty, so far, is the Bahamas. However, the Australian Government has let it be known that it proposes to ratify it and to introduce legislation, during the budget session next month, spelling out the draconian code which the treaty proposes.

Federal Government legislation of this nature may have the effect of overriding State legislation on drug control, including the more lenient legislation in States like Victoria and South Australia. The constitutionality of such legislation is firmly established since the Franklin Dam decision in which the

Federal Government overrode the powers of the Tasmanian Government.

All the political parties are dragging their feet on this question. It is a classic example of the fashionable modern approach which may be categorised as government by opinion poll. Instead of adopting a firm, resolute approach to social problems, based on the best advice available, and then setting out to educate the largely uninformed public to an acceptance of your proposed solution, you commission a public opinion survey and act according to its findings.

Though successive polls have shown a steady shift in public opinion in the direction of the decriminalisation of the use – not the peddling – of heroin, there is no doubt that there is not yet a majority in favour of decriminalisation. That settles the question for our timid policy-makers.

When I first started advocating decriminalisation a few years age, very few people supported me. Today, it is a thoroughly respectable policy with support from some of the most authoritative people and organisations in the community.

This shift in opinion has been caused mainly by the role of the shared needle among intravenous drug users, which is contributing to the spread of AIDS, especially in the heterosexual community. As a result, some of the most vociferous advocates of decriminalisation are to be found among the medical teams involved in the anti-AIDS campaign.

Although the Government appears to be impervious to this changing opinion, it has certainly got through to the backbenchers. A parliamentary joint committee – that is, a committee of both Houses on which all parties are represented – has noted the failure of current policies to prevent the flow of illegal drugs to Australian markets.

It pointed out 'the many myths associated with drug use' and, in particular, a popular misunderstanding about the addictive qualities of some of them.

In its recent report to Parliament, the committee pointed out several policy options and concluded:

The committee hopes that its report will result in an informed debate within the community on these options so that policy development in this area is not left to international organisations and bureaucrats, and so that the policies that are chosen can be clearly demonstrated to be effective in attaining the goals which the community wishes to achieve.

The Fitzgerald Report made reference to the failure of current drug legislation to make any real impact on this major social evil.

The Government does not have the excuse that it is a low priority question. A recent Australia-wide survey showed that the drug problem and government's failure to come to grips with it are the greatest worry of those surveyed.

So what's the hurry about ratifying a United Nations convention that reaffirms and reinforces an approach to this problem which has been discredited worldwide? The only effect will be to set this policy in cement and to postpone the debate which the parliamentary joint committee sought to set in motion.

As long ago as 1971, a report commissioned by the American Consumers' Union found:

The time has come to recognise that heroin is a drug most users go right on using despite the threat of imprisonment, despite actual imprisonment for years, despite repeated so-called cures and despite the risks of disease and even death. Heroin is a drug for which addicts will prostitute themselves. It is a drug to which addicts return despite a sincere desire to 'stay clean', and even success (sometimes enforced by confinement) in staying clean for weeks, months, or years.

This does not mean we have to give up trying, but surely it *is* worthwhile throwing open to the public the question whether the money spent on trying to enforce unenforceable laws and on fruitless propaganda could be better spent on the search for a genuine cure for addiction. In the meantime, take the sleaze out of addiction by decriminalising it and dispensing the drug to addicts under controlled conditions.

The only real purpose I can see behind this rush to ratification is to prove to voters, who will soon be asked at the polling booths whether they would prefer Hawke to Peacock as prime minister, that Bob is getting really tough on the drug problem.

That may win him a few votes among those who ignore the evidence that getting tough on drugs is getting us nowhere. Easily the most ardent supporters of continuing criminalisation would be the heroin black marketeers; they can stay in business only if they are the sole suppliers. The big boys know that attempts to suppress them are nothing to worry about.

28 July 1989

TOMORROW'S POLLIES NEED YESTERDAY'S INSPIRATION

In response to an invitation from a local schoolteacher friend, I turned up last week at a Catholic high school in Sydney's west to talk to a bunch of 17- to 18-year girls and boys in aid of their studies of Australian history. The subject, of which I have some first-hand knowledge, was the Whitlam era.

It was the first time in sixty years that I had set foot in a Catholic school. The atmosphere was quite different to what I remembered of the days of my own Catholic upbringing.

There was nobody in sight in clerical gear, I saw only one small crucifix on the wall, and, *mirabile dictu,* girls rubbed shoulders with boys in a sort of casual acceptance that female and male genders existed in real life as well as in Latin and French grammar, to which they were confined in my boyhood.

I sat down behind a small table and looked out at about thirty young faces. I noticed another change from my own schooldays. Among the Anglo-Celtic faces was the occasional Asian and Middle-Eastern visage, and none of the pupils of Anglo background seemed too Blaineyed about this.

Despite the age gap we were soon getting along nicely, tacitly acknowledging the timeless recurrence of the dilemmas which confront our species.

Australian history didn't rate at all in my schooldays. When I left school I was the full bottle on Agamemnon, Pericles, Julius Caesar, Hannibal, the kings and queens of England and all that European lot, but I had never heard of King O'Malley or Edmund Barton or Henry Parkes. They were the days of the cultural cringe which Bob Menzies – hard as he tried – failed to preserve.

As they sat there, pens poised over pads, the thought struck me that, at the time I was agonising over the refusal of Supply and John Kerr pulling the rug out from under the Whitlam Government, these eager adolescents were mewling and puking in their mothers' arms (or, to put it a little less Shakespeareanly, exhibiting those first signs of 2- or 3-year-old egotism which are dear only to doting parents).

When it came to question time, a confident boy who, I was told, had confessed publicly that Bob Menzies was his hero and role model, stood up and announced: 'It is my ambition to be a politician. What qualities are needed for success in that profession?'

I admired his courage for being game to stand up before his peer group and make such a damaging admission. Undeterred by the titters which greeted his announcement, he obviously had the first qualification for success in politics: a thick skin.

Recently an old friend and I had discussed over a convivial glass the very question raised by this boy. My friend had come up with this unflattering model: a thick-skinned bully, arrogant, articulate, cunningly manipulative, with a good presence (or at least reasonably presentable), self-confident, opinionated, intelligent (though not intellectual), a flexible thinker (ie: a pragmatic liar with a mobile philosophy), egotistical, conspiratorial, motivated, power-driven, energetic.

I couldn't resist the conclusion that he had some specific figure in mind and his model certainly fits some of the more successful politicians of this and other countries.

I fielded the boy's question with a little light-hearted banter along the above lines. However, it occurred to me that to leave this young audience with the impression all politicians are by definition contemptible would be both irresponsible and unfactual.

Success in politics undoubtedly demands at least some of the qualities listed by my friend.

But in politics, as in everything else, fashions change. The current paradigm in Australian politics is the desiccated calculating machine (if I may borrow Aneurin Bevan's rather unjust characterisation of Hugh Gaitskell). Exemplars of this breed, spawned in the school of so-called economic rationalism, are Paul Keating, Peter Walsh and John Hewson.

According to this way of looking at the world, all problems are to be judged by an economic yardstick alone. This sometimes leads to conclusions which are absurd even by economic standards. Thus Keating's recent dictum that we can't have an upgraded infrastructure (that is, we have to learn to live with potholes and different rail gauges) because we can't afford it, will probably condemn us to a worse economic performance than he asserts to be achievable.

Though I would be the last to espouse the politics of the warm inner glow (a phrase which, by the way, I modestly lay claim to having coined) I can't envisage today's youth being fired to participate actively in politics by individuals with the narrowly pedestrian philosophy of today's contenders for the next prime ministership.

As politicians, Ming and Gough had style and wit, as well

as a commitment to their policies (right or wrong). I'd be prepared to wager that they'll be role models for young political aspirants long after today's graceless bunch has sunk without trace.

19 September 1990

A TIMELY REMINDER

Now that Bob Hawke and Paul Keating have belatedly and grudgingly seen fit to confess that our present travail may owe something to their own errors of judgment, is it too much to hope that humility is about to get a guernsey in the conduct of our polity?

I must confess to a fear that their *mea culpas* are based, not on sincere contrition, but on advice from their public relations experts that a bit of breast-beating may just manage to deflect some of the anger of those (most of us) who had already reached the conclusion that they had made a mess of things.

Mr Keating still insists that there must be no deviation from the policies which he has touted as the way out of our troubles, even though such policies have evidently aggravated those troubles.

Mr Hawke threatens the ABC for daring to allow the expression of any views which may be construed as casting doubts on his wisdom in leading us into the Gulf War quagmire.

These are hardly promising portents of an abandonment of their habitual claims to infallibility.

The tone of public economic debate in this country, as set by Mr Keating in his time as treasurer, has been one of uncivil, doctrinaire fundamentalism.

The dogmas of the holy church of economic rationalism have been enshrined as unchallengeable verities. In particular, the doctrine of deregulation is as sacrosanct to Mr Keating as are the virgin birth or transubstantiation to the Pope. Dissent is blasphemy.

I do not presume to assert that the economic theories which have so captivated our treasurer have been definitively proved to be wrong.

But I suggest that it is time he is reminded of some truths which have long been obvious to more highly educated economists than himself.

As Tom Fitzgerald says in one of his recent Boyer lectures: 'Unlike the physical and biological sciences, economics treats the issues that impinge on people's value judgments and personal and class interest.'

Fitzgerald goes on to point out the inconclusive character of much economic inquiry by comparison with the hard sciences, and touches on the tendency we all share to protect our egos by refusing to acknowledge contrary evidence or argument.

Fitzgerald makes no specific reference to the hubris of Mr Keating. He simply reminds us that 'it has become the hallmark of a top-flight economist in recent years to become more modest in his or her claims for the subject'.

He instances the case of Sir John Hicks, a Nobel Prize winning economist who died in 1989 and who, near the end of his life, in Fitzgerald's words, concluded that 'economics could not be regarded as a science but rather as a discipline, a method of tentative and self-critical inquiry'.

He quotes Sir John thus: 'I think it is becoming a vice of economists to overplay their hands, to claim more for the subject than they should.'

I do not know whether Mr Keating or his Treasury advisers have taken time off from the study of their models to glance at Tom Fitzgerald's comments on our present economic plight.

I have seen no response from these dogmatists to his *cri de coeur* over 'the absurd taboo that exists on the discussion of financial deregulation as a significant contributor to our present economic condition.'

We have seen enough of Mr Keating's dismissive hauteur to expect him to give short shrift to Tom Fitzgerald's plea for a little dose of glasnost in the local economic debate.

But perhaps, especially now that proceedings in the House of Representatives are subject to the revealing scrutiny of television, he may find it wise to imbibe a lesson in the civility and urbanity of tone which characterise genuine intellectual discourse.

From now on he will be judged, not just by the applause of his journalistic sycophants, but also by the impression he makes on viewers in the heat of combat. Perhaps that is why he resisted for so long the intrusion of television cameras into the House of Representatives.

Life has become so complex that there is a tendency, fostered by the experts themselves, to accept the proposition that only the experts are entitled to comment on our difficulties.

Once again Tom Fitzgerald, although a formidable economist himself, offers a salutary warning that 'it is a fatal mistake to allow economics to gain ascendancy as though it is not part and parcel of ordinary human life'.

Our more arrogant economic pontificators might also benefit from reflecting on the words of the great Spanish philosopher Jose Ortega Y Gasset, written 60 years ago:

The specialist 'knows' very well his own, tiny corner of the universe; he is radically ignorant of all the rest . . . He is not learned, for he is formally ignorant of all that does not enter his speciality; but neither is he ignorant, because he is a 'scientist' and 'knows' very well his own tiny portion of the universe. We shall have to say that he is a learned ignoramus, which is a very serious matter, as it implies that he is a person who is ignorant, not in the fashion of the ignorant man, but with all the petulance of one who is learned in his own special line.

Remind you of anybody?

20 February 1991

THE FOUL PART OF POLITICS

There are those, I among them, who would assert that to call a public figure a homosexual in no way impugns his integrity or fitness to hold office.

But I would readily agree with Dr Blewett that in the general climate of public opinion in this country, such an allegation amounts to a smear and is intended by those who spread it to harm the target's reputation and do him or her political damage.

There is nothing new about the smearing of public figures. What is new in Dr Blewett's case is his public confrontation of the scuttlebutt. It was a brave and dangerous thing to do since it helps to spread the rumour among people, including myself, who had not heard it.

It is also a welcome change from the knee-jerk reaction of most politicians to issue a writ at the hint of a slur and to jump on to the defamation gravy train.

Dr Blewett is not the first Australian politician to be the victim of this particular smear. After all, in a poofter-bashing country like Australia, it is as inevitable that such an accusation would be damaging as it would be in a Latin country, where machismo is all, to suggest that a man was sexually impotent.

The smear is as much a part of political life as Question Time. It is not based solely on malice, although that is its principal ingredient.

Denigration of one's opponents (not necessarily confined to members of other parties but sometimes including other members of one's own party) is as integral a part of political life as tackling in a game of rugby.

As we recently learned from the British Lions, that can

include some pretty foul deeds. It is also fanned by the boredom of political life and the universal human fondness for gossip. The content of smears gives a valuable insight into a country's mores and prejudices.

When I was in parliament, a couple of prominent Liberals – a man and a woman both with spouses – were seen in each other's company with increasing frequency. We lived in such close propinquity in the old parliament House that our comings and goings were soon common knowledge.

It was not long before it was assumed that this pair were 'on together'. I didn't think they were up to anything more than providing each other with company to assuage the loneliness of life in Canberra for a politician.

But it was interesting to observe that while the man's reputation was enhanced by the general belief that he was 'getting a bit', there was much less tolerance for the woman's supposed infidelity.

Similarly, Mr Hawke's reputation as a womaniser probably enhanced rather than damaged his standing. He didn't need to cry over it.

With the notable exception of Gough Whitlam, there have been sexual rumours and innuendos about most of our recent prime ministers. Such rumours about Menzies were said to have earned him the displeasure of a powerful media mogul, who vented his spleen editorially. Harold Holt was also the subject of sexual rumours, as was John Gorton.

The smear is as impossible to suppress as that other hallowed parliamentary practice, the leak. It is almost impossible to track down the origin of a rumour. As it is passed along the line, nobody asks for proof. Once it has acquired the status of common bar and cab talk, it is stated as a self-evident truth without any need of verification.

Even if a victim of a smear could obtain evidence of one person passing an untrue and damaging rumour to another, a successful action for slander would afford little relief, as the rumour would have taken on a life of its own and would continue to be believed by those who want to believe ill of the person defamed, especially if he or she is a politician.

The findings of the Fitzgerald Commission have enhanced the credibility of the wildest smears of politicians and policemen.

The caution of newspaper editors usually ensures that the smear does not get into print unless, of course, it gets an airing in parliament under privilege.

In the United States, where the laws of defamation offer much less protection to public figures than here, it is a curious fact that presidents have enjoyed during their lifetime so much immunity from disclosure of their sexual habits.

There was a tacit code of silence among journalists about the fact that Franklin Roosevelt had a mistress, while the promiscuous capers of John Kennedy did not surface widely until after his death.

But the aura of reverence which envelops an American citizen once he dons the presidential crown does not extend to mere aspirants for the office, as was shown in the case of Gary Hart.

While I believe that a person who assumes public office should be subjected to the closest scrutiny, I have an old fashioned belief that that scrutiny should stop at the bedroom door.

19 July 1989

THAT OLD FAMILIAR FEELING

I'm afraid I qualify as a mover and shaker. I have none of the accepted credentials of that fashionable condition: I don't operate in the forex markets, I don't drive a Porsche, I don't wear a bimbo on my arm, I don't frequent the dining places where you are sure to be photographed. But the very thought of moving makes me shake.

I am referring, of course, to the traumatic experience of changing one's place of abode. At the time of my most recent move I calculated that this was my sixteenth such performance in the 43 years since I migrated from Melbourne to Sydney. But I have never become laid back about it. There are often compelling reasons why we must do it but the actual experience is always painful.

Mobility of domicile tells us a lot about what sort of individuals we are and also about what sort of society we live in. My parents got married in their twenties and moved to the house in which they continued to live until they died in their seventies. In the years when I was growing up that was the norm.

Between the two Great Wars, Australia was a conservative, static society. In that time it experienced one major disaster, the Great Depression which engulfed the capitalist world and which radicalised a section of one generation. But, by and large, basic Australian social mores did not change much and the essential conservatism of its inhabitants was reflected in our geographical immobility.

Young people tended to remain in the family nest until they got married and they mostly stayed married to the same person. Until the time arrived when ownership of a car became commonplace, they did not even move around their own city very much, let alone travel interstate or overseas.

One of the obvious causes of increased mobility is the decrease in permanence of marriage. On the break-up of a relationship, one or both of the parties move on. I'm not concerned here whether that is good or bad (in my view, it is in the nature of things) but it has been good for the real estate and conveyancing industries.

Another factor is the gradual increase, through widening educational opportunities, in upward social mobility. One of the ironies of history is that the escape from one social grading to a more elevated one, which once induced individual migrations from crowded inner city suburbs now involves a shift from unexcitingly salubrious suburbs to refurbished and yuppified dwellings in those formerly down-market purlieus.

The car, which has changed life in so many ways, has probably been the most important factor in increased mobility. Owning a car opened up abundant choices of places to live and conquered the problem of distance between home and work.

Ultimately, of course, it encouraged the urban sprawl and, another irony, turned the quick journey into the bumper-to-bumper crawl. In its turn, that unforeseen result has contributed to the desirability of living in the old despised inner suburbs.

These are some of the reasons why people are on the move so much more today than they were in my childhood and youth.

In the world beyond our shores, the forced mobility of entire peoples, engendered by wars, famines, revolutions and the inhumanity of tyrants such as Hitler and Stalin has been one of the more poignant manifestations of the turbulence of this cruel century.

But even if you move because you *want* to move, the actual process of moving is always an ordeal. My unease on such occasions has little to do with regret at leaving a familiar neighbourhood, or attachment to a particular dwelling. All that packing and unpacking and the disruption of familiar routines are always a pain in the neck. I've never known anybody who enjoyed it.

More than anything else, I resent the separation from my books during the period of leaving one place and settling in another.

About a year ago my wife and I decided to quit Sydney for a house in the Blue Mountains we had hitherto used as a weekender. We soon discovered that the amenities which had sufficed for a couple of days a week were inadequate on a full-time basis.

So we packed up once more while a refurbishment was undertaken which, we were confidently assured, would make the place uninhabitable for only three months. Nobody who has undertaken a similar venture will be surprised to learn that it stretched into seven months, not to mention the blowout in cost.

For part of that time during the wettest months of last year our not inconsiderable library was stored in a damp spot under the house until we moved the books to a store.

We feared for their condition but, now that they are back on their shelves, it is gratifying to report that only one book was so damaged by moisture that it had to be thrown out. It is even more gratifying to report that it was a Harold Robbins potboiler which had been given to us by someone who confused airport novels with literature.

But even that favour from fortune has not obliterated the horrors of moving. I will wander no more.

17 January 1990

A PLEASANT STROLL IN A CEMETERY

On a recent Sunday, eight of us sat down to lunch in a setting of pleasant ancientry, an old house in the old (by Australian standards) town of Richmond, New South Wales. Four of us were in our seventies and another was nudging.

For all that, the conversation, encouraged by some good wine, can best be described as gay – naturally, in its erstwhile connotation.

It was a radiant autumn day and when we had finished our meal our hostess, one of the relative youngsters present, suggested that we take a stroll around the nearby cemetery.

Some might regard that as a slightly macabre form of post-prandial relaxation for such a coterie. But we fell in with her suggestion and, speaking at least for myself, spent an enjoyable hour among the local interees. (I confess that word lacks the cachet of the *Shorter Oxford* but, since the realm of death is the home of euphemism, I crave leave to substitute it for the harsher term.)

Sure enough, a considerable number of the occupants had dodged the ultimate fate of all living creatures, simply by 'passing away', 'crossing over' or 'departing'. Judging by the inscriptions on the tombs, there had been little doubt among those they left behind that their souls had been transported to their eternal reward.

I suppose it is tautological to refer to a soulless cemetery, since that is what all cemeteries are by definition, at least according to the composer of graveyard prose or poetry.

But there are in the secular sense soulless cemeteries, lacking any benison of style or grace.

You could not say that about Richmond cemetery. It looks down on lush river flats and nestles up against an elegant, lovingly preserved Georgian church. If I may adopt a phrase of the period, it is a nice final resting place.

Though some of the lettering, especially on the sandstone slabs, has been ravaged by time into illegibility, there's still some good reading there. (The more recently bereaved have preferred marble to cover their loved ones, presumably to give the inscription a longer life.)

The skills of the stonemasons of old did not always include literacy. One inscription, almost effaced, bewails the tribulations of the deceased thus:

Affliction soar (sic) longtime bore
Physicions (sic) was in vain.

As I contemplated that homespun lament of yesteryear, a modern version occurred to me:

Paid all his tax, tried every quack
But finally put his cue in the rack.

To convey some idea of the age of this graveyard, one inscription tells us that the occupant was born in 1793, the year of the Terror in the French Revolution. The sacredness of matrimony was then such that death itself was a mere temporary separation. The shared grave was the norm. But then as now, wives had a habit of outliving husbands.

There is one grave whose first occupant, a male, called it a day at 51. His widow did not join him until she was 96. One wonders whether, during all those years of widow's weeds, she stuck steadfastly to the abnegations then expected of a Darbyless Joan.

Grave sharing, for all its sentimental associations, was essentially a forerunner of the modern trend to urban consolidation.

Just as Sydney is running out of ground for people to build houses to live in, the growth in our population is creating a shortage of places of final repose. Our demographic problems embrace both the quick and the dead.

Old graveyards provide small glimpses into the births of commercial dynasties. In a corner of the Richmond cemetery there is a shared grave in which one of the occupants was a Pitt and the other, her husband, a Badgery. Was this the merger (the preferred term to takeover in that gentler era) which set in train the revered firm of Pitt, Son and Badgery? A cemetery is also a good place to study changing fashions in names. You don't run into too many Elizas, Mauds, Reubens or Ezekiels today.

The human tendency to tiptoe verbally around the finality of death can produce some hilarious euphemisms. One day on the Blue Mountains train, an elderly lady who had been sitting silently opposite me was jolted into loquacity by a female coeval who boarded the train at, I think, Glenbrook.

They had clearly not met for some time and a conversation ensued which only a Barry Humphries could do justice to. I had no alternative but to put down my book and share their loudly exchanged confidences.

'How long,' asked the recently embarked one, 'is it since you lost Fred?' That kept them going until Rooty Hill.

And well it might. It seemed that Fred had been lost for

some 15 years. People frequently go missing in the Blue Mountains, but most of them are found within a day. I barely forbore a tear at the thought of poor Fred wandering around the peaks and valleys and gorges in all sorts of weather from blistering to freezing for all those years and God knows how many more to come. Surely it would have been more sensible for Fred merely to pass away.

8 May 1991

IRONING IN THE SOUL

These days I'm something of an iron man. This statement does not signify that I'm about to throw down a challenge to Grant Kenny or any of the other flat-bellied, muscled young men who run through sand as though it were a laundered race track, plunge into a tumultuous surf and swim as though they were in the backyard pool, then run back through the sand aerobically undisturbed.

I mean that I have become a bit of a dab hand at the ironing board. Strongly encouraged by the Bride – who loathes ironing – I have extended my domestic skills to include pressing shirts (including hers) and have discovered it is not nearly such an esoteric skill as I had imagined.

For example, you don't have to remove the buttons first and sew them on again after you have finished. You can actually iron between the buttons.

All parts of the shirt are not equally demanding. You can skimp a little on the parts you tuck into your trousers and, in winter at least, you can overlook the sleeves. Pleats can be a bit tricky but very few male shirts have any. I've even graduated to sophisticated techniques like damping down linen garments before applying the iron.

I do confess that I've had some difficulty with shoulders

but recently a woman friend taught me a special trick to overcome this. I'm looking forward to trying it out next time I pick up the iron.

I used to leave this chore to a marvellous Ukrainian woman, Anna, who included it among her tasks when she visited us once a fortnight. But we moved out of Sydney and out of Anna's range, and the shirts began to pile up.

The Bride issued an ultimatum: 'If you want your shirts ironed you'll have to do them yourself', she said.

Discreet inquiries at a dry cleaners revealed that my fortnightly shirt tally would cost almost as much to launder as purchasing a bottle of whisky. I was not inclined to cut down on my tipple.

Before the feminist tornado hit us, we males used to shelter behind all sorts of alibis to escape our share of the chores. As far as ironing is concerned, we took advantage of women's fear that our heavy touch and insensitivity to fine materials would inevitably result in piles of creased, scorched clothes.

Anna, who became a friend in the course of a couple of years of working for us, paid us a social call recently. She brought with her a female relative from the Ukraine, whose trip is a small sign of the loosening of the straightjacket in the Soviet world.

'You know who does the ironing around here now, Anna,' I asked. She shook her head and I pointed to myself. She translated for her niece and they both dissolved in laughter. They may have glasnost and perestroika over there but I doubt if feminism has stormed many barricades.

I now discover that there are many more iron men than I had thought. When I was doing a little boasting about my prowess in a small gathering of friends over Easter, a contest developed between the males about their respective virtuosity with the iron. What will it come to next?

20 April 1990

THE BURGLAR WASN'T ALL BAD

In some of the more salubrious eastern suburbs of Sydney, I'm told, it is becoming almost unfashionable never to have been burgled.

It's harder to compete for conversational space if your topics are confined to your recent trip to 'in' places like Prague and Budapest, the empty shops of the Double Bay bazaar, the unwisdom of eating oysters in the present state of our waterways and similar earth-shattering matters.

I'm not suggesting that people enjoy being burgled, but they seem to get a kick out of talking about it. Non-members of the ever-growing club of the pillaged tend to feel a bit out of things.

As a three-times victim, I have to confess that these experiences, annoying at the time, have in retrospect acquired a certain anecdotal flavour.

No two burglaries are quite the same. Our first and second occurred in suburban Sydney. The first involved a couple of unfortunate (and incompetent) junkies who were caught in the act and in possession of the stolen goods. For some reason which has always escaped me, they were never convicted.

The second was a highly professional break-and-enter job and the thieves got clean away. The goods were covered by insurance but our real loss was a vase bought in China, to which we were attached for its beauty and as a memento rather than for any great monetary value.

We moved out of the high burglary area of inner Sydney into the sylvan innocence of the Blue Mountains, expecting to be relatively immune to the nastier ways of the Big Smoke. And a couple of weeks ago we chalked up our third heist.

Up here, burglaries (or 'burgularies', the preferred usage in these parts) are not only rarer but rather different.

In a small community your misfortunes are genuinely shared by your neighbours. Moreover, the thieves tend to be run-of-the-mill felons compared with their eastern suburbs fellows, many of whom – I am reliably informed – have degrees in fine arts, the better to work over your antiques.

You soon discover that the mountains constabulary is not staffed by Philip Marlowes or Dick Tracys. There is no call for subtle skills as crime up here is mostly petty and uncomplex. The field of suspects is small, and our investigating constable immediately suspected 'who done it'.

The theft bore the hallmarks of the *modus operandi* of a young local delinquent. The denouement was swift, in contrast to the city where, after you've been robbed you might as well forget about it.

But a doughty couple of women – the Bride and our neighbour the Gardener – decided to pursue investigations. Acting on the theory that the suspect, a familiar figure in our sequestered glades, had no doubt abandoned some of the loot nearby, they sallied forth. Assisting was the Gardener's dog Bob, a beagle-kelpie cross.

Bob tracked the culprit and led the amateur sleuths to the stolen bag and briefcase. All the contents except a wallet were there intact.

The Bride had a quiet laugh over the insurance claim form (now happily scrapped), which asked *inter alia:* 'Have the police recovered any of the items?'

Now it would be antisocial to suggest that a burglary merely provides nice clean fun for one and all and is therefore nothing to be concerned about.

My levity is merely intended to take some of the hysteria out of the discussion in the hope that a rational approach may become possible.

As non-adherents to the present gospel of social vengefulness, the Bride and I experienced a pang of shame that we had, however passively, played a role in sending an alienated youth to a detention centre. We'd have been satisfied if he'd thrown the bag and briefcase back over the fence after extracting the relatively small amount of money he scored.

In any event, in an age of rampant economic rationalism, might we not be laying ourselves open to a charge of wimpery if we were to take sides with those who advocate a vast and expensive attempt to wipe out burglary?

Would not we – like environmentalists, feminists, anti-nuclear agitators, advocates of increased funding for the ABC and similar 'bleeding hearts' – be risking the wrath of Peter Walsh, John Stone and Pope Padraic for ignoring the economic costs of our phobias?

If the burglary trade declined dramatically what would happen to the thriving burglar alarm manufacturers, the people who can turn your house into a Fort Knox, the security patrol services, the insurance industry?

Momentarily embracing the economic rationalist religion I find myself concocting an argument that burglary (except perhaps the corporate kind, which is getting a bit out of hand) could be regarded as a form of redistribution of wealth, a partial privatisation which eased the burden on the welfare system. Being entrepreneurial rather than based on paternalism, it was perhaps not all bad.

To return to reality, I am a bit blasé about all the ranting against such social ills as drug addiction and burglary, to which the former is often related.

They are not diseases in their own right but symptoms of a pervasive social malaise – the alienation of an increasing number of young people from the values of their society. They are reminders of the fact that even the well off are not spared the discomforts of a malfunctioning system. Burglary is the point at which poverty intersects with affluence.

28 June 1990

WHO SAYS INDEPENDENT IS A DIRTY WORD?

How ironic that the dullest election campaign in recent memory (deliberately played that way by both major parties to avoid mention of the pain the winners must inflict) should have such an exciting finish.

Now that I am freed from my self-imposed vow of electoral silence, the members of the greatest growth industry – political punditry – have left little room for further pontification. But there is one question I would like answered: why is Independent such a dirty word to so many of our political gurus? Not surprisingly, the leader of the pack is Pope Padraic I.

In between his daily *ex-cathedra* denunciations in the *Australian* of loony Lefties, loony feminists, loony relics from the anti-Vietnam War era and, most mouth-frothing of all, the ABC, he found time for side-swipes at loony greenies and loony Democrats, and loony Independents.

After the result appeared to be more of Hawke, Pope Padraic referred to the 'absurd Independents, especially Dr Helen Caldicott' and likened her possible election to 'the most absurd political advancement since Caligula's horse'. Killing two loons with one stone, he could not resist adding: 'We won't need the ABC's laboured efforts at political satire any more – there will be the real thing in front of us.'

Max Walsh, on the other hand, who does not lay claim to Pope Padraic's exclusive link with 'the highest authority', stated: 'I suggest Ted Mack is right when he talks about this being the era of Independent parliamentarians.' I, a loony leftover from the Whitlam era, prefer Max Walsh's opinion to that of Padraic P. McGuinness.

The pejorative terms which embellish the disparagements of the Independents are 'single-issue fanatics' and 'political destabilisers'. We are invited to believe that the only quality to be valued in politicians is economic enlightenment (about which there are as many views as there are economists) and that political stagnation is to be preferred to instability.

Just as it was once sacrilegious in the Soviet orbit to question the superiority of one-party rule, there seems to be an attempt here to enshrine the view that for all practical purposes, the contest for political power in a democracy should be confined to two well-established political groupings. To me, that is a reactionary attitude to the dynamism of real political evolution.

In a world of unprecedented change, why should Australia be the only place where political life remains business-as-usual?

It seems to be generally agreed that what distinguished this election from previous ones was the degree of voter disenchantment with both major political groupings.

Instead of bemoaning the emergence of groups seeking to put on the public agenda issues which have been largely ignored by the major parties, I suggest we should applaud such a development as a breach in the Berlin Wall of apathy which has hitherto protected our politicians from the scrutiny of those who elect them.

I have never known politician to be such a dirty word as it is today. That would amount to unhealthy nihilism if the disenchanted merely grumbled and did nothing about it. This time, a large proportion of electors served notice to the established parties that, with apologies to Shakespeare, there are more things in heaven and earth than are dreamt of in their philosophy.

The backlash against the Green movement, the main momentum of which is coming from the economic rationalists, illustrates the resentment of the professionals against the intrusion of amateurs into their domain.

It is a time-honoured but not very reputable debating trick

to discredit an idea by depicting it in its most extreme form. Thus the Greens are often portrayed as romantic Luddites who oppose all industrial development, without which our society will sink into backwardness.

The Green movement obviously does contain such elements, although I suspect that some are merely operating on the principle that, among the hard of hearing, you have to shout to be heard. But as I interpret it, the sensible Green philosophy is that in considering the desirability of any large-scale development real, as against token, consideration must be given to the environmental consequences.

Surely the daily disasters which result from ignoring such considerations justify their campaign.

We don't hear a great deal today about the economic mess to which the multi-party system was supposed to have reduced Italy. This is because Italy is a manifestly prosperous modern country. These smaller parties, in practice, softened the abrasive effect of two major political groupings - each claiming to be the repository of all wisdom, forcing them to absorb into their policies some of the programs of the minor groupings.

An example of this in Australia is the success of Graham Richardson in selling to his party the necessity of incorporating some of the objectives sought by environmentalists. It is immaterial that his conversion was expedient rather than principled.

So I am not disturbed at the emergence of non-conformist individuals with sufficiently appealing policies to get elected to either the State or federal parliaments.

If they turn out not to represent viable social objectives, they will disappear. The best of them will help to fertilise the sterile soil of Australian politics.

They will not disappear merely by being stigmatised as loonies.

29 March 1990

CLYDE'S COMRADES

The Cameron Diaries
by Clyde Cameron
Allen & Unwin, 1990

Shortly after the first federal Labor government in 23 years took office in 1972, I disembarked one day at Canberra airport and was joined by the new Minister for Labour, Clyde Cameron. As we walked across the tarmac to the reception building, Clyde, eyes darting hither and thither to make sure he didn't miss seeing who was talking to whom, espied the imperial figure of the new prime minister.

'Imposing presence, eh?' Clyde remarked, and then added: 'You've got no idea how much trouble we've had with him on the road to power.'

This remark encapsulated Cameron's ambivalent attitude to Whitlam: grudging admiration but, above all, watchfulness. As a custodian of socialist purity and Labor traditionalism, he was constantly on guard against Whitlam's individualism, his tendency to ignore party protocol, his irreverence towards the party's tribal elders ('the twelve witless men').

As a reading of this book will demonstrate, no matter how often Gough's jabs sent Labor's professional guardians of the faith reeling across the ring, Clyde, at least, showed up as a bonnie counter-puncher.

Amateur observers of the political scene fall into grievous error by regarding it as primarily a contest between two competing political philosophies: generally one representing the big end of town and the other purporting to carry the torch for the non-privileged. The fact is that the bloodiest and most interesting brawls occur within the family walls of the contending forces. The pagans, during the early years of Christendom, used to remark in wonder: 'How these Christians love one another!' From the time of my earliest contacts with the Labor movement I have marvelled: 'How these comrades hate one another!'

In his introduction the author tells us that in the 31 years that he was a member of the House of Representatives he always kept a daily diary of significant events and comments made by those with whom he held conversations. Each morning he would make a tape of his notes of the day before and, at the end of each week, his private secretary would transcribe them.

This book, which runs to 868 pages, covers only two years, 1976 and 1977. But there are numerous flashbacks to previous years. The author claims that, apart from deletions of passages that were 'trivial, repetitious and libellous' (how I'd love to read the last!), this book contains an unexpurgated version of his diaries for the years 1976 and 1977.

So I suppose it is only fair to say that the opinions he expressed about people to his diary in 1976 and 1977 may have been modified and softened with the passage of time. In any event, even though Clyde is not a conspicuous mellower, I for one have obviously been released from the doghouse I occupied at the time the diaries were being compiled. I enjoyed a most pleasant lunch with Clyde and his wife Doris in Adelaide recently. On that occasion, he even expressed some affection for Gough! As we grow older, we tend to run out of the steam required to maintain the rage.

Anyone who has been a political practitioner must marvel at the energy and total absorption in his trade which Cameron makes manifest in these diaries. When you consider the branch meetings, the clan gatherings such as national and state conferences, the factional cabals, the constituency lobbying in which he was immersed, how could he also be bothered to sit down day after day to record the minutiae of political life here contained? It made me realise what a rank dilettante I must have appeared to a man like Cameron and to understand the distaste he often felt for someone like me.

Referring (in 1977) to the rigours of his political career he says:

It's been a hard, gruelling 28 years. For the 18 years I was a shadow minister I never once had a holiday. I worked 7 days a week, 365 days a year – Sundays, Christmas Day and other public holidays made no difference. For most of that period I would have averaged 16 hours a day, some days I would work with only 4 hours sleep. For most of those years I never knew what it was to feel tired, either mentally or physically. However, those years of long hours, study, research and writing took its toll and at long last I have to concede I am feeling tired!

I've not always been totally convinced by the boasts of workaholics about their addiction to toil, but I believe every word of Cameron's description of his lifestyle. Contrary to what hedonists may think, I believe that is a description of a satisfying – dare I say happy? – life. For totally obsessed people, there is never a dull moment. Addictions blot out other possible ways of living.

Cameron listened to and recorded every bit of gossip and scuttlebutt which came his way. That much of it was wildly inaccurate I can attest from many of the hilariously incorrect tidbits he records about me. But his comments on me are mostly perspicacious:

There is still speculation that Jim McClelland will beat Ken Wriedt for leadership of the Senate, but I can't see this happening. McClelland is a much better debater than Wriedt and he has panache and presence but Jim is disliked for his aloofness and for the way he bashed the unions when he was Minister for Labour and Immigration [a job Whitlam gave me after bundling Cameron out of it]. *And, another thing, he is* too *competent to be liked.* [His prediction was spot-on. In the contest for leader of the Senate in 1976 Wriedt trounced me 38 to 25.]

It is no wonder that in the long haul, a person who was prepared to take the trouble about detail (which was meat and drink to Cameron) would have the edge on others in factional contests, because of his assessments of the likely behaviour of his colleagues derived from his meticulous study of their habits, strengths, weaknesses and biases.

In the pre-computer age, the information in his files and his memory made him virtually a one-man ASIO. His diary contains information such as: the seating arrangements at a dinner he attended at the New York residence of the Australian Ambassador to the UN in 1976; the wines served at a dinner hosted by David Rockefeller the same year ('a second-rate 1972 Puligny Montrachet and an appalling 1966 Gevrey Chambertin'. Cameron is a wine buff); who probably voted for whom in every election for any important position in the ALP, within living memory (constantly checked, rechecked and revised as more information came his way); Rolf Harris's incorrect interpretation of the meaning of the words of Waltzing Matilda (on which Cameron, as an old shearer, is an authority) at a concert in Carnegie Hall the same year; who was dining with whom on any occasion that Cameron was in the parliamentary dining room (and details of their conversation if he was within eavesdropping range); who bothered to come into the House when Whitlam was making an important speech and who was pointedly absent; the state or reported state of health of a member who might affect the vote in a forthcoming ballot. He never missed an opportunity to improve his dossiers: 'It is usually a profitable experience to sit next to a leading politician's wife or girlfriend. A clever politician will not give much away – even to a very close associate. However, one can always rely upon his wife or lady friend to fill in the gaps.'

One of the pitfalls into which Machiavellians are prone to fall is to attribute over-subtle reasons for conduct which can be simply explained. In the lead-up to the caucus ballot, held on 31 May 1977, to decide Bill Hayden's challenge to Whitlam's leadership of the ALP, there was unceasing speculation as to who would support whom.

Who was down there in the scrum, pushing and shoving and raking at the ball with hands and feet? You guessed it. Even though he didn't have much time for Hayden, Cameron was automatically on the side of anyone who was attempting to thwart Whitlam for any prize.

He couldn't figure out where I stood in this contest. That is understandable because neither could I. At that time I admired Hayden and felt sure that Whitlam could not lead Labor to a comeback victory. But, not being a real politician, I finally decided, quite sentimentally, that I could not bring myself to be a party to the downfall of a titan like Gough, notwithstanding the flaws and blemishes discernible on a close scrutiny of the most distinguished human beings. I agonised over my choice, knowing there would be only a couple of votes in it.

When I reached my decision I went to Gough's room and told him. Bill called around at my room and I told him too and my reason for my decision, which he accepted with grace. If Clyde had asked me where I stood I'd have told him too.

But listen to Cameron, speculating before the ballot: 'Something funny is going on in Jim McClelland's court. Either he has really dumped Whitlam or else he is working overtime to deceive Hayden into the belief that he has the numbers to win when he believes he can't.' My mind never worked like that. Perhaps that's the difference between an amateur like me and a pro like Clyde.

But the crassest error we can make in assessing our fellow human beings is to imagine that anyone is all of a piece and can be slotted into a filing system. This apparently intransigent hater of the mighty of the earth and their apologists and political representatives, has a curious streak of tolerance. He has kind words to say for Tony Street, Fraser's minister for labour; for Bob Ellicott, Liberal attorney-general and hounder of Labor's loans affair principals – Whitlam, Murphy, Cairns and Connor; for Santamaria, the demon of the Groupers; and strangest of all, for those paradigms of

Adelaide's 'master-class', Sir Alexander Downer and his wife, Mary: 'I like Alick and Mary. Alick amuses me . . . Mary is great fun. She likes a joke and is more radical than Alick. One would never guess she is a Gosse-Barr Smith.'

There is much in this book which is pure gossip, scuttlebutt and ephemera. There is a mountain of detail which could be of interest only to a person of Clyde Cameron's passionate absorption in all things political. But to those who, not content with the rather shallow view from the press gallery, would like to know what the squalid, fascinating world of politics looks like from the inside, Clyde Cameron is the man to conduct them on a guided tour.

This should be a basic text book in every school of political science under its proper classification: A Catechism for the Political Professional.

Independent, August 1990

NOVEMBER 11? WHAT HAPPENED?

Another 11 November has come and gone and I must confess that, had it not been for the historical regurgitation occasioned by the need to fill the hungry maw of the media, it might have passed me by as just another day.

I am not referring to the significance of the day as marking the end of the War to End All Wars. In a world where there is always a war going on somewhere that reason for finding the day meaningful is also fading.

But to me, as one who was in the eye of the storm on 11 November 1975, the events of that day fifteen years ago might as well have happened a century ago. Not only have I found it impossible to maintain the rage, as urged by Gough Whitlam to those gathered on the lawn outside the old Parliament House after David (later Sir David) Smith had read his master's proclamation dissolving the parliament. I have also increasing difficulty in recalling the emotions of that day and its aftermath – earth-shattering though they seemed at the time – and indeed, in ascribing all that much significance to the events of the day itself.

I suspect that the actual participants in great historical events are the least reliable interpreters of the significance of such events. For confirmation of that suspicion we need look no further than a much more famous November day.

I am referring to November 7 (by our calendar) which has, ever since that day in 1917, been the commemoration day of the Bolshevik revolution.

The storming of the Winter Palace in (then) Petrograd, which marked the end of the tsarist era, was hailed by its participants as the dawn of a new and enlightened age, when ordinary men and women would no longer bow to tyrants and hunger would be banished forever.

They could hardly have been more wrong.

This year, 73 years after that event, loud cries were heard throughout the land which was supposed to have been set free, for the abolition of the celebration of a day which had, in reality, ushered in one of the cruellest tyrannies in human history.

I am not suggesting anything so dramatic about 11 November 1975. But we participants were wildly astray about its significance and its consequences.

The emotions of the moment misled us into what turned out to be absurd hyperbole.

The more romantic and impressionable believed our 7 November 1917 had arrived.

I recall addressing a protest meeting in Hyde Park shortly after our dismissal and being heckled by a bunch of students for casting a cold douche on their suggestion that all we had to do to overthrow capitalism was to call on the workers to down tools and storm the barricades.

It was widely heralded as the death-knell of the Westminster system of democratic government.

Fifteen years later, that system, with all of its absurdities and anachronisms, is still with us and stumbling along reasonably well.

Well, at least it must have spelt the end of the tie with royalty! Surely Australians would no longer tolerate having a governor-general, nominated by the English monarch of the day, daring to assume a role in the conduct of our affairs by a democratically elected parliament!

This sentiment gave rise to a brief efflorescence of a republican movement and I can recall speaking from the stage of Sydney Town Hall, along with such distinguished compatriots as Patrick White and Donald Horne, to enthusiastic audiences who applauded our urgings for the severance of the umbilical cord with mother Britain. But the great majority of Australians clearly couldn't have cared less and republicanism, as a viable movement, soon withered on the vine.

Who could have predicted in those days that a leading member of the Whitlam Government, who came within a few votes of losing his seat in the election which ensued from the dismissal, a man who had expressed his contempt for the office, namely Bill Hayden, would a decade or so later have his tongue hanging out for the office of governor-general and would be duly appointed to it by the (Labor) prime minister of the day?

And who could have foreseen that the villain of the piece, the bunyip aristocrat Malcolm Fraser, whose contempt for the processes of democracy had provoked the crisis when he sooled on his party to withhold Supply, would be accorded eminent person status by that same Labor prime minister, who would also go touting the members of the British Commonwealth to vote for the same man as the head of their organisation?

And surely the Senate, that unrepresentative political anachronism, would be either abolished or cut down to size by an indignant electorate voting in a referendum?

Today, the Senate is enlarged and has more members than ever in positions of power in the ministry.

I read recently that the members of the Australian Rugby League team on a bus tour of London had some of the scars of the Blitz pointed out to them. 'What was the Blitz?' some of them asked.

'What happened on 11 November 1975, Daddy?'

14 November 1990

LABOR, THE PARTY THAT IS NO MORE

It's about time the Labor Party stopped kidding itself that the grassroots supporters who have deserted it in droves in the past five years or so can be wooed back by gimmickry or window-dressing – they are gone forever.

Graham Richardson, the party's shrewdest judge of political trends, is right in acknowledging that, in the light of the steady decline in membership, 'it's pretty hard to call us a mass party'.

Most Labor leaders, especially those who live in Canberra, immured from the disturbing reality of life in the nation's suburbs, look no further than the polls for an assessment of their standing with the electorate, avoiding, if possible, such sordid chores as visits to their branches.

Is it any wonder that branch members reach the conclusion that their elected representatives, especially if they are Cabinet ministers, are indifferent to their views and formulate policy on the advice of shadowy, non-Labor (even anti-Labor) people?

The soul-searching which has proceeded unabated in recent years in the upper reaches of the party as to the reasons for its loss of traditional supporters seems to me to miss an important point.

That is, that to many rank-and-filers, who stood to gain nothing personally from membership and who were always available to distribute how-to-vote cards on election day, the ALP was not so much their party as their church.

According to this quasi-religious view, it was the repository of the only true answers to the irrationalities and the moral callousness of 'the system'. Even those who never thought of themselves as socialists regarded 'the Party' as their shield against the blows of uncontrolled market forces.

No religion, secular or transcendental, can get by without devils. The Laborites of the period of which I am speaking had the most easily identified devil of them all: the Capitalist System. And even though few of them wanted it overturned, they expected their leaders to limit its capacity to exploit them.

So it is easy to understand their bewilderment in recent years at the sight of the most prominent of those leaders fraternising with people who, to them, are prime exemplars of capitalist rapacity, such as Alan Bond, Warren Anderson, Rupert Murdoch and Kerry Packer.

Paul Keating would dismiss his fondness for the yachts and mansions of the tycoons as irrelevant to the policies he espouses.

But that's not how the foot soldiers of Labor saw it. And, perhaps without knowing it himself, Keating reveals a lot about his real ethos in wanting to rub shoulders with such people.

A few years ago, after I had written something mildly questioning his infallibility, I got a phone call from Keating. In that 'soft, seductive' manner which has been discerned recently by pollster Rod Cameron, he slipped straight into one of his familiar, tongue-lashings. When he paused for breath, I took the opportunity to ask him why he fraternised with the likes of Alan Bond and Warren Anderson.

'I like stars,' he replied. No mention of spivs in those days.

Presumably this fondness for 'achievers' also explains his benign view of the Murdoch press octopus and his dismissal of the recent media ownership rally as 'the greatest lot of hot air I've ever heard in my life'.

The old Labor Party of the warm inner glow was obviously overdue for an injection of economic realism and for the merciful slaughter of a few sacred cows.

If they had been treated less arrogantly by their leaders, a lot of the disenchanted apostates would have accepted the necessary modifications of cobwebbed doctrine.

What they objected to was that the baby seemed to be going out with the bath water.

Keating used to be fond of describing the Whitlam era as 'amateur hour'. Whether or not his own 'professional' style has more or less to offer to the ordinary man and woman, people are correct in adjudging that the traditional Labor Party has gone out of business.

Since ideology became a dirty word and economic management became the buzz term, Australian politics has been reduced to a contest between competing teams of economic rationalists, each claiming to be more economically rational than the other.

(Incidentally, it must be getting almost as hard for the Liberal and National faithful to maintain the rage against their vanishing devil, the wicked socialist.)

With the exorcising of ideology from mainstream politics, religious political fervour is now confined to the fringe movements, such as the Greens and Independents.

The diagnosticians of the anaemia of the Labor branches are overlooking a fundamental rule of the very market place with which they are infatuated.

If a product which has enjoyed a large market share is drastically altered in shape, smell, content, quality and packaging, even sticking to the old brand name won't be enough to guarantee its sale to its old customers. Its manufacturers must seek a new market.

Labor's new-style pragmatists should forget about wooing those who have given it away and seek votes among those who used to regard the ALP as the enemy. A change of name may help.

5 December 1990

FUN? HEY, WE COULD TAX THAT

Those whom the gods would destroy they first make ridiculous. Yes, I know that the last word of that old axiom should be 'mad' but the suggested variation seems more apposite to our present condition.

The gods have had a bit of help recently in the form of a hilarious satire, *The Royal Commission into the Australian Economy,* which has just completed a season at Sydney's Belvoir Theatre. Its talented cast made the most of this zany commentary by John Clarke and Ross Stevenson on the political and economic absurdities of the current Australian scene.

The familiar characters lampooned included: Bob Hawke, virtuoso of tearfulness and sport-worship; Paul Keating with his Saddam-like gift of transmuting defeat into victory; Alan Bond, paradigm of the entrepreneurial snake-oil salesman; special-interest apologists such as Sir William Gunn and Bill Kelty; the strutting egos of the media, personified in caricatures of Geoffrey Robertson (played by Sue Ingleton in the high spot of the show), Derryn Hinch and Peter Harvey (Canberra).

I would have liked a second helping. What about garrulous Gareth, ever ready to give a few thousand words of advice on anything at all to the world's statesmen? And why not make the point that, though this Federal Government may not be the brightest we've had, it must be easily the heaviest. We could have had one or other of those bun-bolting behemoths, Kim Beazly or Robert Ray, intoning Hamlet's words:

'Oh that this too too solid flesh would melt,
Thaw, and resolve itself into a dew.'

It is a well-established historical fact that in hard times

people seek more, not less, entertainment. What is perhaps America's distinctive cultural contribution, the musical, flourished during the Great Depression. It will be a pity if our economists, who have surely done enough already to depress us, are allowed to put a damper on similar gloom-relief today. Yet if David Clark can be taken as representative of the breed, that's what they threaten to do.

Dr David Clark (to be carefully distinguished from John Clarke, co-author of the show) is an academic economist whose weekly column in the *Australian Financial Review* exemplifies the tone of papal infallibility in which economists quarrel with each other and lecture the rest of us. Recently he favoured us with a critique of *The Royal Commission*.

Dr Clark evidently decided that, in the theatre as in every other field of human endeavour, economists are best qualified to guide our footsteps. (Surely the time has come for an economic exegesis of sexual pleasure?)

I was startled by Dr Clark's review when it appeared about a month ago, but I deferred commenting on it until I had seen the show, which was not until the closing night.

After almost shamefacedly admitting he got a few laughs out of it, Dr Clark then got stuck into the show on the grounds of its economic illiteracy. His criticisms – couched in verbiage which suggests that a little literary rationalism would not go amiss – may be summarised thus:

The authors of the show and its producer, Bruce Petty, 'may have been 1960s radicals but their not-so-hidden, hidden agenda political message for the 1990s is highly reactionary'.

One of the advantages economists have over ordinary folk is that they can detect a not-so-hidden agenda where we can't. Unlike Dr Clark, the show's authors, while pointing out the follies of our pollies and others, don't consider it their function to proffer a remedy. Oddly, they regard their task as being to entertain us.

A lot of villains, according to Dr Clark, escaped the ridicule they deserve. (The authors would reply, I expect, that if all the fools and crooks got a guernsey, the curtain would never fall.)

Examples of Dr Clark's villains are: the welfare lobby – 'the Julians in Disneyland or Eva Coxes, and Canberra'; 'femocrats'; 'the funding of the arts and the ABC are obviously still sacrosanct topics' (and still pet obsessions of the Righteous Right); and 'the damage the Coronation Hill and Wesley Vale decisions did to our international economic reputation' (due, of course, to those traitorous saboteurs, the Greens).

The show has even more glaring shortcomings: 'The real wage over-hang argument, the twin-deficits theory and the J-curve are all great subjects for clever satirists but they were never explained, let alone sent up.' Shame on the authors for denying us such laughs!

The Clark school of theatrical criticism would probably blackball Shakespeare's *Julius Caesar.* Its grounds would be that there is no historical support for the claim that a soothsayer warned Caesar to beware the Ides of March. Even if we grant that Dr Clark's less-endearing prejudices have a factual basis, art does not stand or fall on factual accuracy.

In venturing into the field of theatrical criticism, Dr Clark, on his performance to date, is in danger of casting doubt on his right to be taken seriously on any subject. He may even reinforce Ross Gittins's suggestion (*SMH*, April 8) that our main trouble may be our economists.

It may comfort Dr Clark to know that the cast of *The Royal Commission* had his review pinned to their dressing-room wall. It seems they got more laughs from it than he got from the show.

17 April 1991

BENEFITS THAT AGE, ALONE, CANNOT WITHER

'This is the first day of the rest of your life,' read the message on the board outside St Michael's Anglican Church in Flinders Street, Surry Hills. It is not the first time I have seen that message, and it has always struck me as ambiguous. Is it a variation on the old hedonistic adage: eat, drink and be merry, for tomorrow we die; or, gather ye rosebuds while ye may/ old time is still a-flying?

I decided that, since purveyors of eternal salvation are unlikely barrackers for the base pleasures of the flesh, the text more probably meant something like: repent, for the end is nearer than you think.

Whatever way it was construed, it didn't offer much comfort to the decrepit. That morning – I was on my way to the dentist for a repair job on a tooth from which the crown had dropped off – I already felt that I was falling apart. But the morbid mood engendered by that grim little sermon didn't last long. As I am of a generally sanguine temperament, my spirits were beginning to revive by the time the crown was replaced.

On the way home, an attractive teenager stood up and offered me her seat on the crowded bus. I was about to decline out of old-fashioned gallantry but realised that to turn down one of the fringe benefits of my geriatric status would have amounted to a public display of vanity. Being old wasn't all bad and I should make the most of what went with it.

As I sat down, I found myself actually counting the blessings of senescence. The capacity to rationalise our woes is an essential ingredient of the psychological immune system.

The kind of things I regard as real benefits of age include

not have to get up in the morning till you're good and ready; eating and drinking whatever you like whether it's good for you or not (if it hasn't killed you by now, what the hell?); and – in my case – giving up the increasingly terrifying business of driving in today's traffic.

But, in my view, the most obvious benefit of age is being freed from the necessity of being nice to those whom you can't stand.

Of course, another way of achieving that beatific state is to win Lotto. I recall a film, *If I Had a Million*, which examined the imagined reactions of an assortment of characters on being informed they had acquired great wealth.

The only image I retain from the film is of Charles Laughton, in the character of a humble clerk in an impressive office, opening the telegram informing him of his win and, without any show of emotion, walking slowly along a seemingly-endless corridor. At the end of it he pushes open a door. Beyond it, his loathsome boss glares at him for his temerity in bursting in uninvited. Old Charles walks up to his desk and lets him have a resounding raspberry, turns and walks back to his office, picks up his hat and umbrella and leaves the building – forever.

But the overwhelming majority of us never win big lotteries and it is only when old age overtakes us that worrying about the disfavour of those who wield the power loses its point. Until then, few of us totally escape the necessity, in the interests of our own survival, of concealing our feelings about people whose disfavour we cannot afford.

In the course of my various avocations, I have had to tip-toe round some puffed-up egotists who could have done me damage if they had picked up any inkling of my distaste for them. During my brief foray into political life, especially, it constantly stuck in my craw to be ever-polite to some factional kingmakers who not only disgusted but, even worse, bored me.

The realisation that my relationships with people can henceforth be based solely on my authentic feeling for them has been an exhilarating experience. And cocking a snook is fun. To be absolved from the imperative of hypocrisy is the chief bonus of getting old.

It doesn't necessarily have to turn you into a curmudgeon. A great number of people in the world, mostly uncelebrated, are likeable and admirable. It's a pity the mighty don't meet a few more of them and get themselves in perspective.

Age is, of course, a shifting concept. To the flower people of the 1960s, anybody over thirty was a 'wrinkly'. The prolongation of human life which, as well as being statistically attested, is obvious to the observer, has induced a rather more tolerant attitude in today's young, though it seldom occurs to them that old age will catch up with them.

I would not like anything I have said about the blessings of old age to be regarded as suggesting that it is better to be old than young.

I like the story of the two ancient libertines sipping their drinks in a bar. A voluptuous young woman enters and each old boy eyes her surreptitiously. Finally one says to the other: 'Wouldn't it be great to be seventy again?'

11 January 1990

HOW SYDNEY CAN STILL BE SAVED

Paul Keating, as is his habit, tossed the cat among the pigeons last week when he suggested that State governments had largely abandoned the cities to private developers. He concluded that if our cities were to be saved, the Commonwealth would have to step in and play a larger role in urban planning. Such noble sentiments come easily to politicians, who are not called upon to put *our* money where *their* mouths are.

In the absence of a specific head of power in the Australian

Constitution, Mr Keating may find the task of rescuing Sydney from despoliation by the developers a little more difficult than the task which Louis Napoleon set himself to make Paris the city which is, today, Paul's favourite.

In 1853, Louis appointed Baron Haussmann Prefect of the Seine with a brief to do more or less what he liked with the rather messy Paris of that time. The Baron proceeded to rip the guts out of the CBD – and that's how Paris got the Champs Elysees and a lot of its present glories. Some of us would like to see the same thing happen to Sydney, but our political arrangements stand in the way.

Guarding the gate of State and city rights is Alderman Jeremy Bingham, the Lord Mayor of Sydney. He is no Baron Haussmann. He is a successful lawyer specialising in local government law, who has fought many doughty battles for the developers Mr Keating reviles (despite being on very friendly terms with one of the more prominent of these modern visigoths).

Mr Bingham's response to Mr Keating's statements was predictable. He poured scorn on the 'world's greatest treasurer' making a claim to be the world's greatest town planner, and he went on to express his confidence that the planning of Sydney was in good hands.

Well, in the immortal words of Mandy Rice Davies: 'He would say that, wouldn't he?'

To expect harsh words about developers to come out of the mouth of Mr Bingham is like expecting a politician to condemn motherhood.

Earlier this year, Mr Bingham was on the verge of appearing for the property developer, CSR. The company was opposing the imposition of a Permanent Conservation Order sought by the Heritage Council, the National Trust and the Sydney City Council (whose Lord Mayor then was and still is Mr Bingham) on terraces in Mount Street Ultimo, which CSR wished to demolish.

The NSW Law Society had to step in and remind him that its Professional Practice Code states: 'by reason of his executive position, a solicitor who is mayor or shire president should not act against the council of which he is head.'

Mr Bingham bowed to that ruling but there is nothing in his history to suggest that developers are in for a hard time during his incumbency. Whatever may be wrong with Sydney, Mr Bingham would, quite sincerely according to his lights, deny that the finger should be pointed in that direction.

In my view, all that you need to confirm that the developers have been given open slather to uglify the fair face of Sydney in recent years is a pair of eyes.

I recently took a stroll through handsome Hyde Park, entering from the southern end and sauntering under the fig trees in the sweet early spring sunshine. As long as you let your eyes stray only to the right, where they fall on the pure contours of the grammar school in College Street, or further ahead, the Barracks, the Registrar-General's building and St Mary's, your mood can remain buoyant.

But as I passed the War Memorial, I glanced to the left and my gaze was affronted by a glimpse of that ultimate urban bad joke, the Coopers and Lybrand Tower on the corner of George and Bathurst Streets: the one that looks like the Disneyland castle.

What distinguishes it from a hundred other such glass towers in the CBD is that it is baby blue with pinkish brown longitudinal stripes on the corners of its facade and is capped by large obtrusive pseudo-deco excrescences of the same hue.

In short, its banality is two-toned instead of monochromatic. To savour its full vulgarity, it should be viewed from the west. From that aspect, it stands out like the gold tooth of the proverbial flash rat.

I commend to Mr Bingham, without any real hope of convincing him, the words of the French sage Claude Levi-Strauss:

Cities have often been likened to symphonies and poems and the comparison seems to me a perfectly natural one. They are, in fact, objects of the same kind.

The city may even be rated higher since it stands at the point where nature and artifice meet. A city is a congestion of animals whose biological history is enclosed within its boundaries and yet every conscious and rational act on the part of these creatures helps to shape the city's eventual character.

By its form, as by the manner of its birth, the city has elements at once of biological procreation, organic evolution and aesthetic creation. It is a natural object and a thing to be cultivated; individual and group; something lived and something dreamed. It is the human invention par excellence.

I don't doubt that, to Paul Keating, this would be an appropriate description of what a city should aim to be. The growth of cities is in the hands of men and women. Successive city councils of all political persuasions have fumbled the chance to turn one of the best endowed sites on earth into a beautifully functional city in which to live. Despite the developers' mayhem, there is still a bit of Sydney left to save.

It's time somebody else was given a chance to do the job. The French long ago realised that Paris was not just the concern of Parisians but of all the French. The same goes for Sydney and Melbourne at least among Australian cities. More power to your arm, Paul.

6 September 1989

PRECIOUS CITY OF THE SOUTH

According to the more crass local chauvinists, Melbourne is a dull, predictable place where a surprise is the last thing to expect. Not so.

When I was there last Thursday, I witnessed the most original industrial demo in my recollection.

I don't know what the issue was but in the middle of the

day all those trams without which Melbourne grinds to a halt were driven into the heart of the city and abandoned for an hour or so by their crews.

Swanston, Elizabeth, Flinders, Collins and Bourke streets presented the extraordinary spectacle of hundreds of motionless, bumper to bumper, unmanned, unwomanned trams. Their greens and yellows shimmered in the early summer sunshine.

No one seemed very put out about it except a couple of the crankiest cab drivers who have ever driven me anywhere. In any event, how could an inhabitant of any city on earth dare to feel patronising towards a metropolis of such arboreal grace?

If I may be permitted to mix a metaphor, when it comes to trees Melbourne is a city which has put a lot of its eggs in one basket. I'm referring to what is to me that city's principal adornment: its noble elms.

I'm not suggesting that is the only tree that flourishes there. There are also plenty of planes, ash, liquidambars, oaks and, especially along the Tullamarine freeway, some splendid eucalypts.

But, once you are off the freeway, it is the elm which transfigures the main avenues leading into the CBD. It dominates Alexandra Avenue and its surrounding parks on the southern bank of the Yarra.

Above all, those cathedral-like flying buttresses which overhang the walkways of the most beautiful gardens in Australia, the Fitzroy Gardens, are the interlacing branches of ancient elms which have been sculptured skywards by several generations of devoted and knowledgeable gardeners.

When the Dutch elm disease was ravaging the elm population of the northern hemisphere a few years ago (several million elms succumbed in Britain alone) I feared for Melbourne, whose beauty would have sharply depreciated if the virus had struck there. Fortunately it did not cross the oceans.

Melbourne owes more to its trees than any city I know. They

uplift a landscape lacking Sydney's natural gifts of majestic waterways and undulations which enable a large proportion of its populace to enjoy heart-lifting views.

Melbourne's trees play a major role in contending with and camouflaging the ravages of today's Visigoths – the developers.

On a recent visit to Melbourne to promote my new book, I stayed at the Hilton Hotel on the edge of the Fitzroy Gardens in Australia's most elegant suburb, East Melbourne. From my window on the seventeenth floor I looked out across the tops of the trees, mostly elms, to Fitzroy and beyond that the Treasury Gardens, a total space almost as large as the whole CBD.

My eyes finally reached a point on the horizon where trees ceased and the monotonous towers of a modern metropolis began. As in Sydney, the skyline is dominated by cranes and the elevator cores of bigger and bigger architectural banalities.

As part of the publicity campaign organised by my publishers, I was interviewed by a bright young journalist of the Murdoch press and, of course, I had to be photographed for the accompanying illustration.

The pleasant young photographer who had been deputed to do the job arrived at my hotel room and said: 'They tell me you're into elms. I'd like to photograph you standing next to one. Are there any around here?'

We went downstairs, across handsome Clarendon Street and into the Fitzroy Gardens. Within eye range I would estimate there are at least 100 of the most majestic elms in the world. The nearest was some 10 metres from where we were standing. 'Can you find an elm for the picture?' asked the young photographer. I did, and a glory of nature was duly made real by his camera.

I had inspected what was happening to the Melbourne CBD and discovered that, as in Sydney, the developers had done and were still doing their worst.

It was a lovely early summer day, sunny but with a typical chilly Melbourne wind. Though its streets are wider than

Sydney's, the modern towers that blot out the sun are even more intrusive than ours because, on a day like this (and there are many of them there) every sunny spot is precious.

But as I gazed along Melbourne's spacious streets, the crimes of the developers were all but obliterated by the gorgeous light green, brand new foliage of the thousands of trees which softened the contours of the brutal glass towers so dear to the hearts of today's architects and tycoons.

Whenever I revisit Melbourne I have the guilty feeling of the man who has walked out on a worthy woman for a slightly tarty beauty. But I must say that, thanks mainly to its trees, central Melbourne and its nearest purlieus have worn better than their Sydney equivalent.

Dear old Melbourne, on a day like that I love you and don't know why I ever abandoned you.

9 November 1989

ART SUBSIDIES HIGHLIGHT THE THEATRE OF THE ABSURD

Those who have taken an interest in subsidised theatre in recent years may have gathered an impression that sponsorship is on the increase. In the face of shrinking Government support, Australian theatre companies are increasingly being forced to seek outside help – often by matching subject matter to sponsor. Thus we've had stockbrokers backing a play about the money market and Arnotts bankrolling a piece about a wartime biscuit factory.

But the reality is that this kind of backing represents a pitifully small proportion of the income of our theatre companies. For example, in 1988 the Sydney Theatre Company received less than 5 per cent of its income from corporate support.

When it comes to supporting theatre, where are the hot gospellers of private enterprise and the tycoons of *Business Review Weekly's* Top 100, ever eager to proclaim the benefits their efforts bestow on the community?

Even if they lack the *noblesse oblige* of the financial Establishment, surely their PR advisers should bring to their attention the benefits of being associated with a flourishing theatre in a society where they have done so well for themselves.

These reflections were provoked by my attendance last week at a fundraising dinner held by the Sydney Theatre Company. This company over the past decade has brought to the public, in the Drama Theatre of the Sydney Opera House and in more recent times in the Wharf Theatre at Walsh Bay, dramatic productions of world class. But the finances of the Sydney Theatre Company, like all theatrical companies in Australia, are poised on a knife edge.

My association with theatre goes back to a few years' board membership on the old Phillip Street Theatre in the 1950s. Sydney is today richly endowed with theatrical fare, but in those days, if your taste ran to revue or satirical comment on the current scene, you had nothing but the Phillip Street Theatre. It was always on the verge of disappearance through financial inanition, until it folded for lack of a venue, after the old Georgian building in which it had performed was demolished.

Similarly, the Belvoir Street Theatre, of which I was a founding father, has had to fight all the way to stay alive, despite numerous awards for excellence and a national and international reputation as one of the most innovative and exciting companies in Australia. But it's even more difficult to attract support for risk-taking theatre.

In the case of the Sydney Theatre Company, I also have to declare an interest as one of an interim board of three commissioned to set it up.

At the dinner referred to, the outgoing director, Richard Wherrett, cited an instance to demonstrate the financial tightrope walked by that most efficiently conducted theatrical enterprise, whose charter is to mount quality work without charging elitist prices.

For five weeks last June, the Sydney Theatre Company played *Romeo and Juliet* to 91 per cent business in the 544-seat Drama Theatre of the Sydney Opera House. A cast of 17 was the primary factor in a total expenditure of $678 000. The total income was $487 000 – a loss of $190 000.

To those of purely commercial mind, the answer would be obvious: put up the price of admission. But theatrical audiences do not mainly comprise affluent people. There is a price limit beyond which audiences would fall off, thus aggravating, rather than solving, the problem of financing good theatre.

The Sydney Theatre Company, in its 12 years, has mounted 114 productions, 34 world premieres of new Australian works, 11 interstate tours and four international tours. Of its productions 44 per cent are Australian works. It is committed to developing a corpus of Australian dramatic works which in time will be part of our classic heritage. Despite this, only 21 per cent of its 1989 income came from Government subsidy, while 79 per cent was earned by the company.

This is an extraordinarily high figure, compared with, say, Berlin's Schanbuhne Theatre, where Government subsidy is 80 per cent. Even in England, Mrs Thatcher's notorious fend-for-yourself Government subsidises England's National Theatre to the tune of 70 per cent.

It is also worth noting that of the total assistance of $831 000 which the Sydney Theatre Company received from the State in 1989, $689 000 went directly back in rental and salaries for the Drama Theatre.

Today's financial climate is not such as to encourage hopes of increased Government assistance to the theatre. The most vociferous opponents of Government expenditure on 'non-essentials' are the high priests of private enterprise. And of all the arts, theatre in Australia has always been the poor relation and, in terms of private sector backing, its support from business languishes way behind that given in recent years for the pictorial and plastic arts (not to mention sport).

An item in last Monday's *Australian Financial Review* disclosed escalating business support for such art forms in the past three years, despite competing demands for the 'charitable' dollar.

In that period companies have built up collections of largely Australian art. A recent survey, cited in the *Financial Review* article, showed that combined capital and non-capital expenditure on the arts by the corporate sector was running at $59.8 million compared with the Australian Council's annual budget, including administration, of $61 million.

Perhaps the immediate return in prestige of having a Van Gogh or a Rembrandt or even a Tom Roberts hanging in your corporate waiting room is more apparent than being listed in the program as a patron of a particular theatre.

But in terms of a contribution to the quality of life in the city where you have prospered, financial assistance for good theatre is just as socially valuable. It's tax-deductible too.

5 April 1990

MOUNTAINS OF THE MOONSTRUCK

'But how do you fill in your time up there?' I was asked recently by an old boulevardier mate who just can't understand how a quintessentially urban man like me can cope with what he sees as the tedium of life in a place like the Blue Mountains.

Well, there's a lot more going on up here than lowlanders suspect. A handsomely produced leaflet in red and yellow landed in my letter box at the beginning of the month, headed 'What's happening in the mountains in September?'

I was about to throw it away with the rest of the junk mail which is as abundant here as elsewhere, when my eye was caught by the question 'How's Your Blood Pressure?'

Since mine is a bit dicey, I read it and found that if I fronted at a van ouside the K Mart at Katoomba (where I buy my grog) I might have my blood pressure checked, courtesy of the health department of the Seventh Day Adventist Church. No obligation to join, but a nice bait for geriatrics.

I read on and found that, courtesy of the same outfit, I might attend a motivation seminar, at which I would learn 'to make a new start to improve my physical health and mental outlook and reach out with a new lease of life' (tempting, at age 75). The program included films with the sinisterly uplifting titles of 'Lifeclimb' and 'Pack your own Shute'.

Also on offer were morning and evening sessions of a nutrition and vegetarian cooking seminar and a meal. Although I am anything but a meat freak, I share George Bush's aversion to broccoli, and don't have the stomach for a sermon on carrots. I'll also give the Quit Now seminar a miss, since it's directed at the only vice I've ever beaten, smoking.

At the Marvels and Mysteries of Nature program I might 'see the evidence of a creator in the amazing migratory flight of the mutton bird'. On another night, a certain lecturer and photographer will show a few of his 40 000 colour slides presenting 'a Bible prediction stranger than fiction'.

We are informed that '2600 years ago a Jewish slave foretold the downfall of Babylon, Persia, Greece, Rome *and our own modern world*'. I was obviously being softened up for Armageddon. Is it their longing for the beatific vision that makes fundamentalists wallow in doom and earthly horrors?

I was reminded of a story related by Auberon Waugh in a recent *Spectator,* debunking a tale which had been going the rounds that 55 000 human babies were being bred every year in the US for the tables of Satanists. (Obviously a devious plug for vegetarianism.)

The story had been investigated by the London paper, the *Independent on Sunday,* and found to be baseless. It had been invented and spread around by fundamentalist Christians. At least they haven't resorted to anything like that up here.

But why, I have often wondered, if this life is such a transient bagatelle and the next one such a big deal, do they cling so tenaciously to this mortal coil? Why worry about your blood pressure, why eschew such life-shortening substances as meat, tobacco and alcohol?

It must be clear by now that the mountains are not starved of entertainment or uplift. True, what we are offered by our local fundamentalists doesn't add up to a hedonistic romp. (Why, by the way, do they flourish in this purlieu? The Rev Fred Nile polls very well in these parts. Perhaps it's the pure air.)

It is sad to have to report that, despite the hyperactivity of our holy ones, the seven deadlies seem to be doing as well here as elsewhere. Judging by the number of fatties, gluttony has not been put to flight. Quit Now doesn't seem to have had much impact on the abounding puffers. I strongly suspect that little headway has been made in the diminution of tippling and adultery.

Recently, an arsonist has been active in our region. He specialises in setting fire to churches. The more reasonable of us think he is carrying his apparent distaste for God's salesmen too far. Here as everywhere, the flesh is holding its own.

Finally, for guaranteed fortnightly entertainment of the slapstick variety, I can recommend our local council meetings, presided over by a mayor who has just been forced to pay $14 000 in fines which were imposed more than three years ago for his failure to lodge tax returns.

That's hardly what you'd expect in an area where fundamentalists have such a high profile. Ours is an ambiguous part of the world.

□ □ □

'No self-respecting fish would be wrapped in a Murdoch paper.' That is not my own original observation, but I would like to have said it. It was uttered by the famous American columnist Mike Royko the day after Rupert Murdoch bought the *Sun-Times* of Chicago in 1984. Royko, who had written for that paper for years, resigned and was immediately snapped up by the opposition Chicago paper, the *Tribune.*

In the present state of the Australian newspaper world, you couldn't expect a local journalist to say anything like that about Murdoch unless he or she had independent means, had the mortgage licked, and the kids had left the nest. You never know when Rupert will be the only newspaper proprietor left in Australia.

12 September 1990

TIME TO KILL OFF THE DEATH PENALTY

It may seem incongruous that, at a moment in history when a cruel regime has just given the world a fresh lesson in contempt for human life in the massacre of Tienanmen Square, Amnesty International should have launched an international campaign against the death penalty and its reintroduction.

If the rulers of the most populous state on earth, who lay claim to be guided by an enlightened philosophy, can seek to justify the murder of thousands of unarmed citizens demonstrating, not for the overthrow of the government but merely for modest democratisation, isn't it futile to campaign for the abolition of the ultimate punishment for individuals, even of those convicted of the most serious crimes?

I'm sure that cynics, and even many humane people pessimised by the sheer repetitiveness of inhuman behaviour, will write off Amnesty's campaign as quixotic.

I take the opposite view. The time to reassert the noblest human aspirations is at the moment of blackest despair. Any other attitude cedes the field to the tyrants and to the vengeful members of society.

It is a mistake to think that the battle against the death penalty, even in a country with a relatively creditable, though spotty, record for humanitarianism like Australia, can ever be considered to be definitively won.

It is an issue which surfaces in our midst each time a particularly grisly crime, such as the Anita Cobby murder, takes place. In Sydney recently angry crowds were seen waving a noose outside a police station where the alleged murderer of a 4-year-old girl was taken. It could be said that in this country the death penalty is dead but won't lie down.

In New York a few weeks ago one of that city's more vulgarly flamboyant billionaires, Donald Trump, published a full page advertisement in the *New York Times* advocating the urgent reintroduction of the death penalty in that state. He was supported by a senior Republican politician, Pat Buchanan, who also called for the prompt hanging of a youth involved in a gang-style rape attack on a woman jogger in Central Park, (you might well ask: What's so extraordinary about that in New York? Well, you see, the victim was not some faceless black outcast but a white Yuppie investment consultant).

The great metropolitan centres of the world, such as New York and Sydney, where the gap widens daily between those at the top and those at the bottom of the heap and increasing brutalisation of society's victims is one of the consequences, are breeding grounds of violence which are destined to provide more and more gruesome clients. This will be grist to the mill of the bring-back-the-noose lobby, which is always with us.

Every society seeks protection from criminals, but to advocate the death penalty as retribution confuses the issue of justice with the desire for vengeance. We cannot afford to blur the distinction between justice and revenge. In order to condemn and legislate against crime, penal systems must strive to take a higher moral ground and must be built on a different set of values from those they condemn.

Despite centuries of experience with the death penalty and many scientific studies of the relationship between that penalty and crime rates, there is no convincing evidence that it is uniquely able to protect society from crime or meet the demands of justice.

Later this year the United Nations General Assembly will be invited to consider introducing an international legal standard covering the death penalty, which currently is the only human rights issue not incorporated in international law.

The Australian delegation to the United Nations Commission on Human Rights has lobbied hard to see the formulation of a draft international treaty aimed at abolishing the death penalty world-wide and preventing its reintroduction. In Australia this Second Optional Protocol to the International Covenant on Civil and Political Rights will be effective, if ratified, only after the Federal Government enacts domestic legislation.

The protocol calls for a firm commitment on the part of ratifying states to abolish the death penalty, at least in peace time. In abolitionist countries, the Protocol will prevent reintroduction.

The text of the proposed Second Optional Protocol will be sent to governments inviting their comments by the beginning of September before going to the United Nations General Assembly. Once it is adopted by the General Assembly it will be up to individual governments to decide whether or not to ratify it.

Although no retentionist country would be obliged to ratify the Second Optional Protocol, its adoption by the United Nations General Assembly would add considerable weight to the legislation in those countries which are already abolitionist. It would also serve as a further impetus in those countries which are considering abolition.

Now, more than ever, the Australian Government needs to argue the case for the protocol with dissenting governments and persuade such governments that the death penalty is an anachronism and an act of cold blood which diminishes the dignity of a state with pretensions to being considered civilised.

When she was in Australia recently, the chairperson of Amnesty International Dr Franca Sciuto stated: 'Australia is known around the world for its efforts to have the United Nations adopt an International Protocol abolishing the death penalty. The human rights community is looking to you to impress upon other governments the sanity and the humanity of this position.'

The time has come to abolish the death penalty once and for all. This state-sanctioned instrument of brutality was described by Albert Camus as: 'The most premeditated of murders to which no criminal's deed, however calculated it may be, can be compared.'

Complacency in Australia that the death penalty could never make a comeback here is as dangerous as the uninformed enthusiasm of those seeking its restoration.

16 June 1989

FEDERATION DAY, YES, BUT NOT IN THIS MORONIC MONTH

On Australia Day I offered a drink to an old friend who had dropped in. 'No thanks', he replied, 'I never drink during January.'

Since he is a jokey chap I thought he might be playing some sort of prank on me. I couldn't recall whether we had been in each other's company on any previous January day, but he stuck to his guns and I respected his resolution, quaint as I found it, to decline a drink.

Not that I was drinking to celebrate the day, since one day's as good as any other for me to have a drink. But my friend's abstinence did raise a question: have we really any reason to celebrate Australia Day?

Well, I dare say Sydney has, although I couldn't understand Nick Greiner's indignation that the feeling was not nationwide that such celebration should be held on the actual day in the month of January when Captain Arthur Phillip landed at Sydney Cove in 1788.

It will be remembered that the bicentenary celebrations in Sydney on 26 January 1988, aroused far more enthusiasm here than in other States for the simple reason that it just was not the 200th birthday of any place other than Sydney.

If there is a national day surely it is the day when, after more than 100 years of bickering over all sorts of trivia, the six separate States finally came together as a federation on 1 January 1901. That union had been delayed by parochial brawling as to whether Melbourne or Sydney should be the national capital, resulting in the creation of an artificial monster called Canberra, Australia's greatest mistake.

In fact, there's a great deal to lament about Australia Day. It is certainly no day for the Aboriginal Australians to rejoice. It was also the beginning of the process of bringing six separate colonies into being, so dooming us apparently forever to be the most over-governed country in the world. We now have nine governments (including that ultimate farce, the ACT). A good case may be made out for the proposition that we would be best served by one central government and with certain purely local matters administered by regional authorities.

To expect that change to emerge is to entertain the wild dream that a few hundred State politicians will vote themselves out of existence.

Of course, Australia's birth as a white, or British, or European, nation could not have happened simultaneously all over the continent. But the circumstances of that birth as a colony of a great imperial power produced the result that further settlement of other parts of the continent was dependent on decisions of the 'Mother Country' rather than on natural, organic growth from the place where it began.

Thus separate colonies with separate governments owing allegiance to the Crown were gradually established in what became the capital cities of the States, which insisted on preserving a residue of powers even after federation.

So, on balance, I don't see much to celebrate on 26 January or the following Monday, where that is considered more expedient. If we must have a national day, and I have no principled objection to the notion, there are cogent reasons why it should not fall on the actual anniversary or indeed in January at all.

For reasons primarily of climate January is Australia's most moronic month. It is not for nothing that it is known as the silly season. A large proportion of the population is on holiday and the national religion, sport, is celebrated as a combination of a mardi gras and a holy festival.

This year the customary January outbreak of sport mania has been aggravated by the strident, illiterate, jingoistic outpourings from radio and TV sets about the exploits of our athletes at the Curry-Kenny games in Auckland. I have nothing against sport except the notion which is widespread in this country that there is nothing under the sun of comparable importance and that a nation's standing in the world is to be estimated primarily by the competitive achievements of its athletes.

As to the suggestion that Anzac Day should be our national day, I recoil with horror from the proposition that that day be regarded as anything but a day of mourning. On Australia Day this year an editorial in this paper asserted that Anzac Day 'is the day most Australians recognise as establishing, through sacrifice, a national identity'.

While in no way belittling the heroism of the men who died or who emerged alive from what was an act of criminal military folly on a level with the Charge of the Light Brigade, my reaction to even the mention of Gallipoli is one of anger, and incredulity.

It was the ultimate example of colonial grovelling that our political and military leaders allowed our troops to be thrown into that slaughter at the behest of British politicians (including Churchill) and military commanders. It was an adventure which had no chance of succeeding and which was, in any event, an incident in a foolish, unjustified war which achieved nothing except to sow the seeds of another and greater bloodbath.

So by all means let's have a national day which may be appropriately called Federation Day. And let's have it in a time of the year which is less mindless and hedonistic than January in the hope that people's thoughts may be directed to the things about which it is possible to feel some justifiable patriotism instead of jingoistic self-inflation.

Despite the obvious and manifold flaws in the Australian way of life, we do have things to be proud of. As we survey the chaos in so much of the world, we also have reason to be glad that our isolation, despite its obviously limiting aspects, has so far preserved us from so much suffering which is almost taken for granted elsewhere.

31 January 1990

BIG BROTHER IS WATCHING, AND WAITING

Anyone who thinks that the idea of an identification card, enabling Big Brother to keep a tag on most of our activities, is dead should take a close look at the 1990 Budget papers.

We all know about bracket creep, the process by which our taxable income is inexorably pushed by inflation into a higher taxation bracket, guaranteeing that our tax bill goes up.

Let me introduce you to an even more sinister form of the art: function creep. It requires a little bit of explanation but it is really quite simple.

Remember the Australia Card? The idea was first floated in 1985 by bureaucrats enamoured of the idea of having a social register equivalent to a fingerprint bank. Flushed with the unprecedented third successive victory of a Labor government in 1987, Mr Hawke and Mr Keating set out to capitalise on widespread and justified public indignation about tax evasion and welfare fraud. The only effective way to stamp out these abuses, we were told, was to issue an identity card to every Australian (dubbed the Australia Card).

A healthy public outcry against the card's potential to be an invasion of people's privacy, and some clumsy drafting which placed its legality in doubt, ultimately forced its abandonment.

The joint select committee set up to consider the desirability of introducing the card had recommended strongly against it.

When the Government's attempt to flout this recommendation hit the fence, it then adopted the committee's taxation-specific option of an enhanced tax file number scheme.

In announcing the introduction of this scheme in May 1988, Mr Keating gave this assurance: [The tax file number] will not establish a citizen identification system . . . The Tax Office will be the only government agency which uses the tax file number for the purpose of identifying and registering its client base.'

The select committee had warned that if such a measure were enacted, it 'be strictly limited in its terms so that it applies only to taxation purposes, and that those purposes be so framed as to prevent a progressive extension of the ambit of the bill'.

Underlining his democratic respect for the electorate's fears of governmental invasion of privacy, Mr Keating, in his second reading speech on the bill on 1 September 1988, reiterated his earlier pledge in these words: 'No other government or non-government agency will have access to the Tax Office file number registration system, nor will it be able to use an individual's [tax file number] for any registration system of its own.'

[Unemployment and sickness beneficiaries were included in the tax file number scheme because they received Government benefits already deemed to be income for the purposes of the Taxation Assessment Act.]

The rubbery quality of these undertakings soon became apparent. An amendment to the Social Security Act in December last year provided an object lesson in function creep; that is, the gradual augmentation of the original, limited purpose of an enactment.

By this amendment, the Department of Employment, Education, and Training was given access to tax file numbers to administer (i) the Higher Education Training Scheme (a tertiary education fee paid by way of additional tax after graduation) and (ii) the Child Support Agency, to help in the collection of child and spouse maintenance.

Finally, we arrive at the Budget papers, in which the Minister for Social Security, Senator Richardson, announced that there would be additional uses of the tax file numbers.

He later spelt these out to include the following classes of people: sole-parent pension recipients; family allowance supplement recipients; family allowance applicants; age and invalid pensioners; and recipients of payments under veterans' affairs legislation, the Students' Assistance Act and the First Home Owners' Scheme.

Where will this function creep stop? How can the police and ASIO be logically excluded from using tax file numbers if even the administrators of the First Home Owners' Scheme and AUSTUDY are allowed to use them?

And when can we expect that master of the alibi, Mr Keating, to step forward and explain that the gradual and continuing erosion of his 1988 assurances about the limited application of the tax file number scheme is really a confirmation of those assurances, just as he hails every failure of his economic policy as a victory?

It is surprising that the public reaction to the Government's proposals has hitherto been so muted. I have seen a wishy-washy press release from the Opposition spokesman on Social Security, child-care and retirement income, Senator Alston, but his side of politics does not have a history of defence of civil liberties sufficient to inspire much confidence that it will put up a real fight on this issue. If and when it gains office it would probably like to have the powers now being sought by an increasingly authoritarian Government, without incurring the odium of having to legislate for them itself.

The fight will probably be left to the Democrats and such organisations as the Council for Civil Liberties and the Australian Privacy Foundation. The proposals for widening the ambit of the tax file number scheme deserve the same fate as the Australia Card.

5 September 1990

CAPITALISTS CANNOT AFFORD TO CROW

Four men described as the world's high priests of capitalism recently made well-publicised appearances in Sydney and Melbourne, sponsored by some employer organisation, to celebrate the victory of their favoured system over their former competitors, socialism and communism.

It had the flavour of a Leagues club celebrating the winner of the Winfield Cup.

They were: from England Bernard Levin, columnist on the *Times*, and Paul Johnson, historian and columnist on the *Spectator*; and from the United States, columnist Michael Novak and author Robert E. Tyrrell jun. (Why are American fathers so loath to give their sons first names that distinguish them from dad? Sometimes, when they put the first, the second, the third, etc, after their monickers, they sound like a royal dynasty. Perhaps that's the idea.)

I would need to be almost cretinous to deny that recent events in the communist world have shattered the pretension of Marx and his acolytes to have the answers to the social and economic problems of the masses. Their nostrums have left the patient sicker than he was before.

That has been implicitly conceded by Gorbachev in his adoption of policies which sound capitalistic, smell capitalistic and can safely be called capitalistic. The fact that he is compelled, as he was this week on national television, to mouth a few Leninist cliches in order to mollify those who cling to the old, discredited faith should not be allowed to cast doubts on his own clear-sightedness.

It is a time-hallowed tradition for tired ideologies to be invoked in defence of policies which fly in the face of their discarded precepts. The butchers of the Inquisition justified their atrocities in the name of Christ, just as Deng justified the slaughter in the streets of Beijing in the name of Marx.

While not for a moment disputing the historical rejection of the Marxist prescription for social and economic health which we are now witnessing all around the world, my reaction to the gloating of the capitalist Gang of Four came close to nausea.

Britain's unemployed fluctuate between two and three million. Thatcherism has succeeded in erecting a Berlin Wall between the prosperous south of England and the squalid north. On the most charitable estimate, the US has at least two million citizens who sleep in the streets every night.

Here in our backyard, the Government is worried when unemployment falls below 6 per cent because that suggests the 'overheating' of the economy has been cooled down. I don't know how many people detect the irony of the admission that, to be healthy, the economy needs at least 6 per cent of its employables permanently out of work.

In short, it seems to me that it is hardly a time to be celebrating the 'victory' of capitalism.

That said, this may be an appropriate time to try to identify the basic flaw which has terminated the saleability of the 'Marxist solution'.

With due respect to those 'desiccated calculating machines, the economists' (if I may appropriate Nye Bevan's put-down of Hugh Gaitskell) every economic theory is ultimately based on a philosophy of the nature of man (women aren't considered when economic theories are being propounded). The core of capitalist theory is that the motor of progress is greed, although it is usually called by a softer word which does not scratch the tongue, such as incentive.

The idealistic basis of Marxism has been obscured by the cruel practices of the tyrants who have ruled in its name. While capitalism is based on a sour view of the nature of the human species, Marxism was based on a view that men and women are basically rational creatures capable of building a humane, rational society.

'From each according to his capacity, to each according to his needs', the slogan under which the Bolsheviks launched what ultimately bacame one of the most cruel regimes in history, was a noble, but, as it turned out, hopelessly unreal vision.

Trotsky, the Billy Graham of Marxism, expressed it even more apocalyptically when he predicted that under socialism, the average human being would approximate to a Marx, a Goethe or an Aristotle, 'and above that plateau new peaks will rise'.

Despite the Marxists' rejection of all supernatural faiths, I can't see why anyone who can believe that should find any difficulty in swallowing the miracle of the loaves and fishes.

The idea that in a collectivist, totally planned society, people would be so nobly motivated as to give their all with relative indifference to their own personal, material return, was shown to be a pipe dream. So did the tenet that under socialism, its superior productivity compared with the anarchic, unguided efforts of capitalism would result in such a glut of material goods that there would be no jostling at the trough. That most obvious fact of Russian lore, the queue, has put paid to that false hope.

The system bred scarcity and scarcity begets corruption. As is now emerging, there have been plenty of cheats and spivs in high places, including Brezhnev's son-in-law, and Deng's son. When there is not enough to go round, socialists are no more immune than capitalists to the temptation to find ways to get around the system. So they found their own Cook Island rorts.

But the failure of Marxism to deliver the goods (and it ultimately boils down to that) does not, as the Levins and the Johnsons would have us believe, lead to the ineluctable conclusion that capitalism has the answer to the way we should live our lives. It is better than communism, but it is still possible to believe that there may be something better than either.

Perhaps society may evolve in a direction which is not contemplated by dogmatic adherents to either of the present models. There may even be some convergence which will eschew the worst flaws of both. I don't think there will be any 'victory' to claim. Neither side, on its record, deserves an outright win.

And even if the heroes of the new society fall somewhat short of a Marx, a Goethe or an Aristotle, I'm reasonably confident they'll be a little more admirable than a Bond, a Packer or a Murdoch.

14 September 1989

DOUBTS STILL LINGER OVER BUTHELEZI

In my brief career as a columnist, I have enjoyed getting up the nose of a few local panjandrums but I never anticipated that one of my raspberries would ruffle the feather of a foreign head of government.

Imagine my surprise when a letter arrived on classy notepaper, impressively emblazoned with the letterhead: KwaZulu, Ministry of the Chief Minister, Economic Affairs and Police. It was signed by Mangosuthu G. Buthelezi, the bearer of the above titles and, as though that were not enough, the president of the Inkatha Freedom Party.

With courtly politeness, the chief dissented from my categorisation of him in an article in these columns as 'little more than an Uncle Tom collaborator with the white oppressors' of South Africa's blacks.

He undertook to send me a copy of his autobiography and a book by a former assistant editor of the *Cape Times,* Wessel de Kock, which would explain 'just where I come from, politically speaking'. These books, respectfully inscribed, have now arrived. I have read them and offer my comments.

But first of all, how did a passing crack from an obscure antipodean scribbler come to the chief's attention? Has the embattled Fairfax group been conducting a circulation drive in the bantustans (homelands) of South Africa? Perhaps a local representative of the South African Government, whose stooge I had accused him of being, had sent him a copy of my slur. Or perhaps the chief is the one person in the world with a more comprehensive clippings service than Gerard Henderson.

It has become increasingly difficult to keep up with the

changing names of newly independent African States. So the first question which arises is: where and what is KwaZulu? The answer provides the key to the opprobrium attaching to Buthelezi's name in militant anti-apartheid circles.

KwaZulu is not a State in the commonly accepted sense. It is an entity created by the South African Government in furtherance of its apartheid policy. It is a 'self-governing' bantustan of 3.6 million hectares, comprising several disparate chunks of the province of Natal in the south-eastern quarter of the Republic of South Africa. It roughly approximates what was once known as Zululand. The powers which it and other bantustans exercise are those prescribed by a South African Government statute and are hardly greater than those of a municipal council.

Buthelezi became chief minister of KwaZulu in 1970 and by that act, in the eyes of radical anti-apartheid forces, joined the ranks of their enemies. He is, as his biographer keeps harping, 'a prince of the Zulu nation, a scion of the royal blood'. He is a devout Christian who enjoys both classical music and Frank Sinatra; he is in his early 60s and is married with seven children. At university he made friends with Nelson Mandela (with whom he is still on good terms and whose liberation he long advocated), joined the Youth League of the African National Congress (ANC) and came under the influence of the African icon, Albert Luthuli, the president of the ANC from 1952 to its banning in 1960, and winner of the Nobel Peace Prize that year.

The biography, which Buthelezi assured me was not written at his prompting, is unabashedly hagiographic in tone. But read together with Buthelezi's own account of his philosophy and motivations, it comes close to providing a justification for his political stance.

Buthelezi can show that, both in person and through the Inkatha Freedom Party (claimed membership 1.3 million), he has over a long period opposed apartheid at all levels.

He calls the homeland policy a policy to 'balkanise' South Africa by dividing blacks into ethnic groups, separating them not only from white politics but from each other, making them, through 'independence' (which he has rejected for KwaZulu), foreigners in 87 per cent of South Africa.

So why did he join the system? To fight apartheid from within, to use KwaZulu as a base from which to erode the homeland policy, he says. This he calls 'participatory democratic opposition to apartheid'.

At this point, even though he claims to have had the approval of both Luthuli and Mandela for this tactical move, I am beset by a niggling doubt. How did the robes of chief minister of a politically insignificant 'parliament' enhance his value as a freedom fighter?

The fact remains that he is the leader of the largest ethnic group in South Africa, the seven million Zulu people. The cornerstone of his policy, which puts a chasm between him and the ANC, is his total rejection of violence against the white government (although his own tribal followers have been among the most violent in the feuding with other tribes - and even with dissident Zulus). He also rejects the charge that his refusal to join forces with the ANC is based on a determination to be 'the only bull in the kraal'.

He is also anti-socialist (because, he says, socialism does not work) and anti-sanctions because he believes their burden falls most heavily on the poorest.

Like each side in the Gulf War, he is sure God is on his side. He has some harsh things to say about the radical chic which seems to draw the South African clergy, such as Archbishop Tutu, and other people into the arms of the ANC, where the Marxist tail allegedly wags the dog.

For me, Buthelezi remains an ambiguous figure.

1 May 1991

P.S. The subsequent disclosure that Inkatha has received large secret subsidies from the white government has blown apart Buthelezi's disclaimer of being an Uncle Tom.

July 1991

BUSH AND HISTORY'S HARSH FOLLY

Wars rarely turn out according to plan. Since George Bush and his advisers were not smart (or concerned) enough to foresee and forestall the mayhem which their victory over Saddam Hussein would entail for the Kurds, the Shi'ites and other anti-Saddam subjects, this may be a suitable time to draw up a provisional balance sheet of the Gulf War.

Who were the winners? Well, George Bush was one. He was applauded even by members of Congress who had been opposed to his war, his popularity shot up to 90 per cent, and the next presidential election seems to be already in the bag.

Most Americans felt like winners when their President assured them: 'By God we've kicked the Vietnam syndrome once and for all'. The legend of American invincibility had been restored.

But a warm inner glow doesn't last forever or pay any bills. When the euphoria has cooled and the huge scale of the United State's domestic problems can no longer be swept under the rug by victory headlines, a lot of Americans may ask what their 'win' was worth to them.

The Kuwaitis, whose 'liberation', was what it was supposed to be about, already have their answer: torture and slaughter during the Iraqi occupation; burning oil-wells which will take years to extinguish and get back into production; and oppression as before by their familiar despots, murmuring, as they have for years, about introducing a little democracy.

What of the Iraqis? The death toll alone during the period of warfare has been estimated at more than 100 000, plus the wounded and unquantifiable material damage. And then, the real 'mother of all battles', the civil war fanned by Bush's sooling them on to revolt.

What Bush wanted was merely a quick (dare I say 'surgical'?) military coup and Saddam Hussein's replacement by a less-discredited thug, who would preserve the Iraqi State intact but, unlike Saddam, would know his place in the international scheme of things.

Can the Kurds, Shi'ites and other dissidents be blamed for interpreting Bush's urgings as containing an implied promise of assistance?

I take no joy in recalling my prediction early in the war that 'after oceans of blood, as well as rivers of oil, have been spilt, Saddam will probably still be there'. Even if he is supplanted by a CIA stooge there won't be any liberation for the Iraqi people.

Having broken Iraq's capacity to take on a real opponent, those who decide US policy obviously prefer to have Saddam (or his equivalent under a different name) in power rather than risk some new, unpredictable Iraqi government. Better the monsters you know . . .

And, of course, the US's allies in the Gulf adventure would veto United Nations approval of interference in a nation's internal affairs. That would be a dangerous precedent – especially to the USSR and China. This was known to the American leaders from the outset.

Bob Hawke was a winner – for a few weeks. After he had committed Australian forces even before being asked to the venture, he overtook and passed John Hewson in the popularity polls. Last week's Morgan Gallup poll showed he had dropped 7 percentage points since the previous poll, and now trailed Hewson in popularity by 38 to 47 per cent. The fruits of brown-nosing the Yanks are short-lived.

The Americans have made it clear they will toss no rewarding bones to lapdogs. Australia's contribution to the 'allied' cause earned us no favours from the Yanks in trade relations. They have continued to undermine the sale of our commodities in world markets by protectionist cosseting of their own primary producers. So much for gratitude and the 'level playing field.'

The ecological damage of the war, affecting not only the Middle East but in varying degrees the whole planet, has been assessed by experts as being in the Chernobyl class.

And what of the new world order which, we were promised by the American propaganda machine, would follow victory? Will the Middle East become a more stable region? Already, Western armaments are again pouring into the countries whose credit is good.

The lesson that Saddam Hussein's capacity to bully and terrorise the region was made possible only by the West's readiness to supply him with the most sophisticated weapons seems to have been forgotten even before the final cease-fire agreement has been signed. The Arab–Israeli conflict remains unresolved, and no plans for its resolution have emerged. Will a permanent army of occupation in the Middle East be needed to maintain a semblance of order? Is that what new world order means?

I doubt that the US has really 'kicked the Vietnam syndrome'. Is the humiliation of a superpower by a backward peasant nation (as in Vietnam) erased by a crushing military victory over another small, even though more formidable, foe? The reality is that, blinkered by a short-sighted and unimaginative view of its own interests, an American government has once more blundered into a war which, far from enhancing world stability, has immensely exacerbated the tensions which make future wars inevitable.

The great American historian Barbara Tuchman has remarked (in *The March of Folly*): 'A phenomenon noticeable throughout history regardless of place or period is the pursuit by governments of policies contrary to their own interests'.

The Gulf War may well turn out to be a textbook example of that persistent folly. Ultimately, there may be no winners at all.

10 April 1991

THE KURDS HAVE TV ON THEIR SIDE

We have just had another lesson in the power of television. I refer to the threatened Kurdish holocaust, which has probably been averted – or at least postponed – largely because of TV's prying eye.

I am not suggesting that what has happened and is still happening to the Kurdish people fails to satisfy the tests of a major catastrophe, even in a world where the scope and degree of human suffering seem to be subject to a law of inevitable escalation.

But if there had been no TV, I believe the Kurds would have been the victims of genocidal slaughter in the same class as the Armenian massacres of 1915. It is estimated that 800 000 Armenians were killed by the Turks in that pogrom.

Saddam Hussein's record suggests that, in circumstances he deemed propitious, he would not baulk at similar slaughter of the Kurds. He had already subjected them to bacteriological weapons (supplied by the West) with little more than muted American criticism. That was when he was fighting the Iranians, who had been out of favour with the Americans since their puppet Shah had been deposed. Saddam then enjoyed a status based on the old axiom: the enemy of my enemy is my friend.

Those who have watched George Bush's lips while events have unfolded contrary to plan will have noticed these unscheduled shifts in his position:

First: Even when Saddam's helicopters began bombing the fleeing Kurds whom Bush had sooled on to revolt, he said the US would not intervene in the internal affairs of Iraq.

Second: A few days later, he agreed to send material aid but reiterated his determination not to get involved in a civil war which he dismissed as a mere continuation of something which had been going on for centuries.

Finally: He fell in with the proposition first advanced by British Prime Minister John Major and committed US forces to establish protected camps for Kurdish refugees in northern Iraq.

Bush looked particularly sullen when grudgingly announcing this about-face. Why the change of mind?

It is less likely to have been due to a sudden surge of pity than to a realisation that the massive sufferings of the Kurds had penetrated, via television, the homes of the American people. The pro-Bush euphoria which had followed General Schwarzkopf's victory was being rapidly dissipated, just as public support for the Vietnam War had been eroded by the TV coverage of the sufferings of that conflict.

Americans, prone to orgasmic jingoism at the sight or mention of their flag, are nonetheless kind-hearted. The sight of ill-clad fellow humans, including thousands of infants, struggling up bleak, inhospitable mountains, many dying in their flight from their monstrous pursuer, induced a not-to-be denied demand from Bush's electorate that he do something about their plight – now.

The full bill for the Gulf War has not yet been presented but enough has emerged to ensure a large question mark against Bush's place in history. If the multiplication rather than diminution of the problems of the region which the war has wrought is left to one side, the costs to date in lives, material destruction, environmental damage and money are out of all proportion to the aims the war was supposed to achieve.

Anyone who questioned whether it was worth sacrificing lives to prevent Kuwait being ruled by a new tyrant rather than the one it had, was told that, if Saddam was not taught a lesson, he would invade Saudi Arabia and we'd all have to pay much more for oil. This was a revival of the discredited domino theory. Remember, we were supposed to be in Vietnam to stop the downward thrust of communism, which would otherwise engulf us all. As least, that's what Bob Menzies told us. The Americans (and Australians) lost that war but nothing of the kind happened.

No evidence has been offered that Saddam intended to invade Saudi Arabia. Indeed, there has been no official refutation of the claim that he invaded Kuwait only after being misled by an American ambassador into believing the US would turn a blind eye.

War, especially modern war, should be a last resort. That's what diplomacy is supposed to be all about. Now the rashness of American policy, based on a simplistic view of the protection of American interests and a failure to take account of what should have been seen as the inevitable consequences of war, has made likely a long-term presence of US forces in the Gulf. Short wars have a way of turning into long wars and New World Orders have an eerie resemblance to Old World Orders.

The final blow was the unforeseen collapse of the strategy of news management by which the US Government sought to ensure that Americans and the world would know about the war only what it wanted them to know.

The long-held belief that the defeat in Vietnam was contributed to, if not caused by, critical reporting had produced a determination to censor the reporting of the Gulf War by restricting news to that supplied by the Army's spokesman. The TV war thus emerged as almost bloodless.

But TV coverage of the Kurdish catastrophe was beyond the control of the US Army. The resultant desanitisation of the war and its consequences forced George Bush's hand. Thousands of Kurds who would otherwise have perished will now survive. Let's stop cursing the soaps and the commercials for a while, and give a cheer for TV.

24 April 1991

IS THE TOUGH GUY IMAGE WORTH IT?

'Let's make no mistake about it. There's a quiet but very great majority of the community firmly behind Mr Yabsley.' With those words, a correspondent concluded a letter to this paper last Friday and I regret to say I fear that his assessment of public support for the NSW Minister for Corrective Services may be right.

The same assessment has obviously been made by the State Opposition, or rather, in the way that all political 'principles' are formed today, by its public opinion pollsters. How else can we explain the muted (to put it at its most charitable) reaction of the ALP to Yabsleyism in all its forms? Law and order has become a motherhood issue with bipartisan support. Anything resembling charity towards law-breakers, based on a humane comprehension of the forces which breed criminality, has never, in my experience, been at a lower ebb. The vengeful school has elbowed the rehabilitationists aside.

The lower orders of journalism, both print and electronic, must bear a heavy responsibility for the ascendancy of this attitude. The public is constantly invited to wallow in the details of the more horrific crimes, with cameras lingering lovingly on pools of blood, and relatives, in their moments of extreme grief, being prodded into support for bringing back the noose – or even the lash.

The reintroduction of the death penalty for the worst crimes has majority support, despite the evidence from those parts of the world where it is still in force that it is not a successful deterrent. The dire social consequences of the prohibition of alcohol in the United States in the 1930s have also been lost on today's heroin prohibitionists.

The abject failure of expensive and widely trumpeted antidrug campaigns allows the heroin black market to flourish, and the epidemic of muggings and burglaries, which result from the consequential expensiveness of addiction, brings more and more law-abiding people into personal contact with crime.

Mr Yabsley knows he is on a political winner in pandering to the retributive approach to criminal offenders engendered by these forces. As Auberon Waugh remarked on the English scene in a recent column in the *Spectator*: 'The demand for sending people to prison is like the demand for free medicine. There can never be enough prison places to satisfy it or enough staff to administer it.'

In a recent interview with the *Independent Monthly*, Mr Yabsley is reported as saying: 'I would like to be remembered as someone who's put the value back into punishment.'

Without venturing into the marshes of such Christian virtues as pity, forgiveness and compassion, considered so wimpish today, it is worth pausing to cast a cold eye on Mr Yabsley's prospects of fulfilling that ambition. Looked at purely from a value-free, cost-effective, economic rationalist point of view, I would suggest that the prognosis for the success of Yabsleyism is not good.

Consider the principal ingredients in his penal doctrine. First, let us look at the consequences of 'truth in sentencing', meaning the (non-parole) sentence you get is the sentence you'll serve, without hope of remission. The inevitable result is overcrowding of already inadequate places of detention. NSW, with 143 per 100 000 people in jail, has the highest State rate of prisoners. Overcrowding breeds violence, rape, brutalisation. When inmates of such detention centres are ultimately released, isn't it logical to expect more hardened criminals in the community? The alternative is to spend millions of dollars of public money on more jails. Either way, society loses.

Second, in the name of making it more difficult to conceal drugs in cells, prisoners are deprived of the few possessions which alleviate the deprivations of prison life. We have already seen the results of this campaign: uncontrollable riots, bashings and costly destruction of State property. (Why not a methadone program for prisoners and a more efficient way of preventing the smuggling of drugs, including by bent prison officers?)

Third, confrontation instead of negotiation. I have been assured by a psychiatrist, who visits one of our major jails every week, that the overwhelming majority of inmates are reasonable and can be persuaded to accept changes considered necessary by the authorities. He is confident that an acceptable reduction of personal possessions could have been negotiated with prisoners and the recent riots averted.

He has also been authoritatively informed that, without any prior consultation with prisoners, a system of compulsory AIDS testing is soon to be introduced for all jail inmates. He predicts that this will trigger even greater riots than we have yet seen. And yet, this psychiatrist maintains, a system of voluntary AIDS testing could be sold by persuasion to almost all inmates, so that forcible testing would be confined to a few intractables, who would then find no mass support for riotous behaviour. His opinion is based on twenty years' experience as a prison psychiatrist - slightly superior qualifications, one would have thought, to those inculcated by Mr Yabsley's sheltered, yuppie life.

Leaving aside all consideration of the well-being of prison inmates, it is difficult to discover any benefit to the people of NSW in the destruction of our jails at the cost to taxpayers of many millions of dollars, merely to gratify Mr Yabsley's hankering after the reputation of a political tough guy.

17 October 1990

YABSLEYISM VIEWED FROM THE INSIDE

Close readers of this newspaper may have noticed a letter, published last Friday, signed P. Frecklington, Goulburn Segregation Unit. I also got a letter, signed a week earlier, from the same man and on the same subject: the folly and futility of Yabsleyism as a means of asserting official authority over prison inmates, on which I had recently written a column.

His letter to me commenced: 'As a regular reader of your column, the above (ie: my piece on Mr Yabsley and the jail riots) was later circulated, by fair means or foul, throughout the segregation unit here, and from the inmates, en masse and in a word: "thanks".' (I have his permission to name him as the author of the letter.)

Judging from its tone, Mr Frecklington is a very different human being from Mr Yabsley's – or indeed most people's – stereotype of a person doing time.

His letter to me was articulate, witty, ironical, devoid of self pity: 'The individual indignities heaped on me are of little moment. I have suffered worse, am an old "crim" and expect little better.'

How his letters, either to the editor or to me, reached their destination is a little mystifying. I would have thought that especially at a time when the jails are in a state of Yabsley-induced uproar, the censor might have been more vigilant. But, as my correspondent drily remarked: 'There is more than one way of skinning a cat.' Perhaps not all of the prison authorities are in agreement with Mr Yabsley's methods, and enjoy hearing them denigrated.

I am, of course, aware that most people reading this article will take the view that I am naive, irresponsible or (worst offence of all in today's climate of hard-headed pragmatism) a bleeding heart, to listen to and publicise the criticisms of officialdom emanating from a self-confessed criminal.

But my own observation of the moral tone of public life in this country induces me to accept, despite its provenance, Mr Frecklington's comment: 'This vastly inexperienced minister, with the tide of public opinion behind him, a glib TV image and complaisant media, is doling out misinformation which is being swallowed as if it were mother's milk – hiding all but the tip of an unruly, mistreated iceberg – and he must be stopped.' (I can even forgive the mixed metaphor.)

What I find most disturbing, in the wake of the jail riots which caused millions of dollars of damage for which taxpayers will have to foot the bill, is the speed with which the state of our jails and their inmates has become a non-story.

The damage which has been done is much more serious than the mere destruction of property. Mr Frecklington declares, and I believe him, that relations between warders and prisoners 'are worse than the Bathurst riots [1974] – being more widespread – and almost as bad as the "Grafton days".' As he asks ironically: 'Object achieved, Mr Yabsley?'

What is frequently overlooked by proponents of the social-vengeance theory of incarceration is that the overwhelming majority of prisoners will sooner or later be released into the mainstream of society. Their state of mind will inevitably be affected by the treatment they have received and observed being meted out to others during their period in jail. If that treatment has been unjust, brutal, spiteful – as it has been during the Yabsley regime – there will be an increase in the tab the public will have to pick up in the form of random acts of violence and vandalism.

Nor has my intelligent correspondent failed to notice the deafening silence of the Labor Party on the crisis in our jails. 'Heaven forbid that we wait for . . . the "Opposition" to stop dragging its feet – the Labor Party now champions only popular causes.' Presumably, if Labor was in office in NSW, the policies espoused by Mr Yabsley's shadow, ex-policeman

Peter Anderson, would not differ markedly from those of his predecessor.

I do not know for what crime or crimes Mr Frecklington is being punished. Without in any way attempting to whitewash him, which he certainly does not attempt to do himself, the image of him which I draw from this letter is not that of an unreclaimable outcast but of a man who would still be capable of making a real contribution to society.

(Incidentally, I am indebted to my correspondent for correcting my false assumption that there is no methadone program in NSW jails.)

7 November 1990

THE VIEW IS DIFFERENT FROM A HOSPITAL BED

There is nothing quite like a personal crisis to expunge the woes of the world from the front page of our consciousness. At the moment that Stormin' Norman Schwarzkopf's troops were 'liberating' Kuwait I was being lifted onto a bed in the Blue Mountains District Anzac Memorial Hospital, Katoomba, and an oxygen mask slapped on my face.

The only reminder I had that at that moment gallons of human blood were being spilt over the sands of Araby was half a human finger standing in a glass on a shelf opposite my bed. The owner of the other half of the finger, who had himself performed the amputation by closing his car door on his digit, was lying on the adjoining bed with a consoling wife holding his other hand.

My plight was occasioned by a massive asthmatic attack. I have been a chronic asthmatic for many years but my condition had been aggravated by a serious chest infection.

It might not have been a brush with death but it was at least a disquieting tap on the shoulder.

I am aware that this is a mere droplet in a sea of suffering and somewhat less than a matter of general interest. But since my predicament set in train for me a course of events, not earth-shaking but perhaps of some wider significance, I thought I would set them down during my convalescence.

A hospital is a place where people in various states of debility find themselves in graduated conditions of dependency on people they would ordinarily pass and be passed by in the street without either noticing the other's existence. I am not referring to the doctors, who, of course, are the generals of the field of battle for survival, but on the supporting troops – the male and female nurses, the physiotherapists, the dispensers of food and drink, the cleaning ladies etc.

You are soon filled with wonderment that your well-being matters so much to them. Of course, the main ingredients in your recovery and survival are scientific skills and pharmacological substances. But never short-change the human contribution.

As soon as I was up to something more than just drawing breath, I looked around for something to read. My choice fell on a collection of Bernard Levin's columns in the *Times* and the *Observer* and I came upon a column he had devoted to a distinguished former colleague, Patrick O'Donovan, who had spent a lot of time in hospital before he finally died of a prolonged illness.

This is what O'Donovan had written:

Illness can be an insult and a degradation. Pain can reduce a man to the level of an animal creeping into a corner. Nurses practise the sort of naval discipline that is fundamentally reasonable and which is designed to sustain humans faced with horror and filth and inhumanity. They have, like sailors, to face an unnatural situation and love itself is insufficient in such a predicament . . . As long as I was conscious someone told me all the time what was happening. Someone touched me with just the right sort of unsentimental and affectionate respect for a body in a vile predicament.

I was never in a state as bad as that, but from the way I was treated I have no doubt that, if I had been, I would have received similar ministrations.

A stay in hospital is also a humbling experience in other ways. You are suddenly jolted out of your own smug familiar cocoon into a world of people of different backgrounds, education, social status whose only reason for being in the same place at the same time is their common temporary helplessness.

The first night, as I lay struggling for breath in the intensive care ward, I became hazily conscious of a person being wheeled into the ward on a trolley and lifted onto the bed opposite me. In the morning it transpired that he was a young man in a diabetic coma. He gradually emerged from his fog and was visited by his wife, a jolly, sustaining young woman accompanied by two of their infant children.

When he was being discharged a few hours later she was counselled by the medical staff to superintend his prescribed medication more closely to avert another crisis which would involve his readmission. Her difficulty, she admitted uncomplainingly, was that they did not have a fridge in which to keep his medicines. They were returning to their home in a caravan park which they shared with their four children – and a dog.

As I recovered, gazing out through a window while the traffic roared indifferently down the highway and Mount Solitary emerged from its haze in the distance, I talked about their own lives to those tending me. The Gulf War inevitably got a mention. None of these habitues of human distress expressed any other reactions to the slaughter then proceeding than sorrow and compassion for the victims of *all* sides of the tragedy.

13 March 1991

THE EERIE SOUNDS OF SILENCE

My wife and I recently had an eerie experience. The early spring sunshine had tempted us into making a foray into the Hunter Valley. We drove up the wattled Putty Road to Singleton and then into the heart of wine country, finishing near nightfall at one of the many unpretentious, attractive resting places which now abound in the region.

This was, as we had planned, within easy reach of a good eating place with an abundant choice of the noble wines of the district.

We sat on the veranda of our *pied-à-terre* and gazed at the soothing landscape as the light faded. At almost the same moment, we both became aware of something strange. 'Isn't it quiet?' To put it in modernspeak, we found ourselves in an unaccustomed low-volume situation. Not a sound of any sort; no screeching of brakes; no abusive imprecations; no burglar or car alarms; no police cars or ambulances; no rock music from an adjoining apartment; no phones ringing; no bar-room cacophony.

We were suddenly experiencing that pleasure celebrated in the 1960s by Simon and Garfunkel, *The Sounds Of Silence*. And we both found it a bit weird. The feeling of peace was delightful but we couldn't deny that it seemed to be outside the natural order of things.

The capacity of human beings to accept as the norm some awful state of affair which has gradually crept up on them is nowhere better exemplified than in their acceptance – as something to be endured or even enjoyed – of reverberation, stridency, shrillness, the siren, the hooter, the piercing, the stentorian, the ear-splitting, the blaring, the fortissimo (to avail oneself of just some of the variations of aural intrusion proffered by *Roget's Thesaurus*).

My hearing has already undergone a certain degree of senile diminution of acuity but sometimes I wonder whether the hearing of younger generations will survive as well as mine.

At the cinema, the sound level is often so high that it appears to be deliberately distorted so that you can't hear the dialogue. I have seen people putting hands over their ears trying to sort out some recognisable sounds. And Walkman radio cassettes are frequently turned up so loud that you can hear the sound 'leaking' from one being worn by your neighbour on the bus.

I don't know when this passion for noise started, though I think the Beatles have a lot to answer for. I remember taking my kids when they were very young to a Beatles concert at the old Rushcutters Bay Stadium when the Liverpudlian group was at the height of its fame.

Such was the hysteria they engendered among the young that the moment they appeared on stage, or in this case the ring, the audience began to scream and did not desist until well after the concert was over. I did not hear a note of music. When the noise was at its most deafening, I turned to my young daughter and shouted: 'What did you come here for, to listen to the music or to scream?' She replied: 'To scream'.

So I don't suppose it's surprising that when, as I occasionally do, I take the same now grown-up daughter to a restaurant, any conversation is conducted at about the same decibel level as that Beatles concert. In fact, in most restaurants, people are screaming at each other. They are competing not only with Muzak and fellow screamers but the decor of the restaurants – tiled floors, terrazzo-topped tables – which seems specially designed to ensure that anybody wishing to be heard should be equipped with strong lungs and be prepared to use them at full capacity.

It hardly makes for subtle, civilised exchanges. Wit and wisdom are poor competitors with the enveloping clangour. Why waste your efforts? I suspect that may be one reason for the vapidities which today often pass for conversation.

A hearing expert on ABC Radio opined that we are breeding a generation of people whose hearing is doomed to be impaired by industrial noise, rock music and other auditory horrors of our times. The higher frequencies and fine distinctions of sound are beyond those so affected. For example, the dominant sound they would hear in the *1812 Overture* would be the drum. The main melodic theme would come through only as a faint, tinny background noise.

He warned of the aural damage which could ensue from constant addiction to earplugged noise and suggested that the level of sound at rock concerts was considerably above the accepted danger level. Industrial deafness is in fact a hazard of rock musicians.

The accepted wisdom has been that becoming 'hard of hearing' is just one facet of the ageing process to which we just have to become resigned. However, research among remote tribes in Africa and inhabitants of the outer Hebrides suggests that this is not necessarily so.

But, for the inhabitants of modern cities, it seems that through their daily exposure to noise levels which the ear is not biologically built to accept, they are destined to a more rapid deterioration of hearing than in the past.

The ear has many delights. I hope that the growing realisation of the perils of unquestioned 'progress' may reach those whose ears can still pick up the danger signals.

28 September 1989

DOWN IN THE DUMPS ABOUT SLACK RECYCLING

This week I propose to talk about garbage. I mean the real thing, not the metaphorical kind, a lot of which has been written and spoken recently about the Gulf folly by presidents, prime ministers, politicians, pontificators, pamphleteers, pub prophets and (sorry to run out of alliteration) cab drivers. The subject needs no more punditry from me.

Once, garbage was something to which we gave little thought. Insouciantly, we chucked everything into our battered rubbish bins or burnt it off in the backyard, unwittingly compounding landfill problems and assaulting the ozone layer.

Now we know better. Garbage – and the disposal thereof – has become a science, and we've all had to learn the new rules.

In our household, the process has been assisted by the Otto, a tall solid plastic cylinder on wheels issued (at a price) by our municipality to all householders. The Otto (known affectionately by its brand name) is collected automatically by a municipal garbage vehicle whose two mechanical arms adroitly pick up the bin and tip its contents into the masher.

I understand identical or similar bins are used in various municipalities, though not in some inner suburban areas where narrow streets would make the pickup operation impossible. Much more capacious than the old style of rubbish bin, the Otto is an unobtrusive dark green colour, is virtually dog-proof (an important consideration in a doggy area) and, is moreover, manufactured in Australia, being thus suffused with virtue as well as utility.

The Otto is not without its difficulties. For a start, it has to be placed in a precise position beside the kerb with the wheels facing one's dwelling in order to make the pickup operation possible. There is an interdiction on hot ashes and liquids. And it is a labour-saving device since it eliminates the man who used to run alongside the council truck to empty the old-style bins.

Don't get me wrong. Rationality has not yet won the day in garbage disposal in these parts. For the aware consumer, the Otto is not the ultimate solution to the Garbage Problem, especially if you are into recycling. Then you have to subdivide garbage (apart from what goes into the Otto) into six groups: paper, plastic, aluminium, clear glass, coloured glass and vegetable matter for the compost heap (of which more later).

The pickup day for recycled matter comes but once a month in this area, so you will understand that by the end of the monthly cycle, the area under our house has begun to look like something that would gladden the heart of Steptoe and Son.

The amount of newspapers, magazines and junk mail which we accumulate in any month is frightening. And as soon as you put those papers out, you can count on a powerful westerly to disperse them all over the district unless you put several heavy bricks on top. Or it will rain, and a soggy mass will wait the pickup vehicle, which may not arrive for several days.

Recent reports that waste paper is being used as landfill, because the recycling movement caught the paper industry with its pants down and it is unable to process all the waste paper, make us wonder if it is worth the effort, separating the paper from other garbage and saving it up.

If you are fond of a drop of wine, as we are, the bottles, too, mount up to an embarrassing level. I hope those passing our place on the second Tuesday of the month understand that we have friends who help us build up the number of empties.

Our council does not collect plastic bottles or aluminium

cans, the preferred containers for much beer. We have to take the latter to a repository some distance away, and as for the former, it seems the nearest collection place is at Camden!

Again, there are rumours that millions of bottles are piling up because of a lack of reprocessing facilities. And all this sorting and storing of recyclable materials require storage space that not everybody possesses.

It all adds up to a picture of public awareness being well ahead of the capacity and willingness of the authorities and manufacturers to provide facilities for simple, well organised recycling.

Finally, let me come to the laudable little exercise in private enterprise down at the bottom of your garden: the compost heap. I have found that this can provide yet another fertile field of domestic friction.

A certain fanaticism manifests itself in dedicated composters. The Bride reacts very sharply if I carelessly include animal wastes or (horror of horrors) cigarette butts in the compost bucket.

All those layers of umpteen different substances - potato peelings, orange skins, any detritus that started life in the soil, with hay, organic fertilisers and soil itself - make a mixture which is great for your vegetable garden.

Unfortunately, possums like the compost too, and we have found that its proximity to the vegetable garden leads to the inevitable: no vegetables. We're working on that one.

As someone once said, life was not meant to be easy. Especially when it comes to garbage.

22 August 1990

NOBODY CAN BE AN ISLAND THESE DAYS

For the sake of identification let's call him Herb. And, in the name of charity, let's call him elderly rather than old.

Herb lives with his wife in what the Americans call a condo (short for condominium) but which we call a strata title unit.

This means he has legal title to part of the building including a communal garage.

His apartment is on the first floor of a residential development of 80 apartments of various dimensions with a landscaped area and a common caretaker.

The major appeal of these apartments is their proximity to the city and their security.

There is off-street parking with an electronic opening device for each car owner, a special key for the lift from the garage, a common front door key to the building and two different keys to open the front door of your own apartment.

Being close to the inner city, it is an area in which there is a high risk of burglary but with all that security if you get robbed it's bad luck.

But the greatest risk is that you'll lock yourself out.

And that's just what happened one day to Herb.

His wife had left early, intending to return late in the afternoon.

He didn't ask where she would be during the day although he would concede that, being a little inattentive these days, he might have been told but had forgotten.

Herb, as is his wont, rose late, had a leisurely breakfast while he read the papers, had a shower and a shave, got dressed and decided to go downstairs for the mail.

He knew he had his keys because he always carried them

in the hip pocket of his trousers. Wasn't he wearing the ones that he had worn yesterday and had hung over a chair in the bedroom before going to bed?

As he reached the row of letter boxes, his hand went to his hip pocket. Nothing there. His keys were in fact at that moment lying on the bedroom floor where they had dropped from his trousers.

As it had been warm in the apartment, he was lightly clad. He soon realised it was bitterly cold outside.

Moreover, it suddenly struck him that he had forgotten to put his denture in his mouth.

Not to despair. He rang the caretaker's bell. No answer.

It transpired later the caretaker had had a mild heart attack and had been carted off to hospital carrying his master keys with him.

All was not yet lost. For just such an emergency Herb had left a set of keys with friends who lived about two kilometres away.

Fortunately he had the price of one phone call in his trousers.

He walked around the corner to a public phone, which, of course, had been vandalised. By walking another block, he finally found one in working order and rang his friends.

There was a message on the answering machine that they had taken a trip to the country and would not be back for some days.

As Herb stood pondering what to do next, it began to rain. By now he was chilled to the bone and was flapping his arms about to warm himself.

He must have been a strange sight because the deros of Taylor Square hailed him as one of their own. At least, he thought bitterly, they have the price of a drink.

All he could think of was to make his way back to the apartment building and wait at the entrance to his wing until a neighbour who was on the way out could let him into the common lift area inside.

He took the lift to the first floor hoping a neighbour would come home and ask him inside until his wife returned. None did, so he sat outside his own door.

There, five hours later, his wife found him wet and shivery.

This is the moment to confess that what I have just written is a piece of fiction or, to be more exact, it records a personal nightmare.

But the worst possible scenario for a dweller in an urban fortress, embodied in Herb's ordeal, provides a parable for our times.

If you live in Herb's reasonably comfortable circumstances you will be presumed to own the gadgets without which life today is considered unthinkable – radios, TV set, a VCR, perhaps a computer and fax machine, all of which, being easy to carry and to flog, are at the top of the list for expert sneak thieves who just *must* get a quick fix.

And if you own a car, which like most car-owners, you need to park in the street for at least part of the day and possibly also at night, it will be at risk of being stolen or more likely stripped of its radio and other detachables.

So, increasingly, we are impelled to live in bunkers. The ever-mounting insurance you pay on the contents of your dwelling and on your car can really be regarded as a tax imposed on those who manage to find a place in society for themselves by those who, for one reason or another, do not.

I'm not suggesting there's anything new about burglary. But the ranks of burglars have been swelled by a new breed of compulsive thieves. Only a short time ago the legalisation of heroin was considered unthinkable. The spread of AIDS, especially to the heterosexual community, via the shared hypodermic syringe, has put this question squarely on the social agenda.

Its urgency is reinforced by the indirect levy which is imposed on the whole community by the prices that junkies have to pay for heroin on the blackmarket.

When the Englishman's home was his castle, citizens were able to leave it to the authorities to put a moat between them and their would-be despoilers. Today nobody, no matter how smug or indifferent to the fate of society's misfits and casualties, can be immune to the infections or the depredations which it is in their power to inflict.

Never was it truer than today that nobody is an island.

14 July 1989

JUSTICE BY JURY SYSTEM THREATENED

Is the jury system, hitherto considered the very cornerstone of British (and, by inheritance, Australian) justice on its way out? A recent decision of the NSW Court of Appeal might be seen as another step on the way to the jury's grave.

In 1989 a jury awarded to a Sydney solicitor, Nick Carson, a record verdict of $600 000 against John Fairfax & Sons for defamation in the *Sydney Morning Herald*. Most lawyers to whom I spoke at the time considered the sum excessive, and the Court of Appeal has now expressed its agreement with that opinion. In the words of Justice Michael Kirby, the sum was 'not just high but out of all proportion to the circumstances of the case'. The case will be retried, but only on the question of damages.

Such trials are a considerable drain on the public purse. The last one occupied five days and when the process has to be repeated people are inclined to suggest that a jury trial is a luxury we can no longer afford and that the delivery of justice should be left to the judges.

In England, its birthplace, the jury is under even sharper attack. A headline in the conservative magazine the *Spectator* (July 6) reads: 'The jury is an ass'. That stricture is based on the acquittal of two men charged with having helped a spy, George Blake, who had been sentenced to 42 years' imprisonment, to escape from Wormwood Scrubs Jail and thence to the Soviet Union. They were put on trial after 25 years had elapsed only because 110 Members of the Commons, egged on by the editor of Rupert Murdoch's notorious gutter tabloid, the *Sun*, had signed a motion that they be prosecuted. Despite the two men's self-proclaimed guilt and the directions of the judge, the jury refused to convict them.

The *Spectator* fulminated: 'Alas, our juries are increasingly incapable of any thought at all. The jury system is based on the presumed ability of ordinary people to tell right from wrong and to sift an argument. This presumption is false, at least in England: any educated person who has done jury service returns from it appalled at the level of cerebration of his less educated fellow-jurors.'

But hold on a minute. Conceding the undoubted perversity of some jury verdicts, surely it is a horse laugh to suggest that a just verdict is guaranteed if the decision is left to the judge. Not only are trial judge decisions regularly reversed on appeal; even appeal judges differ among themselves, as they did in the Carson defamation appeal. One of the three judges of the Court of Appeal dissented from the majority decision and would have allowed the record verdict to stand. It is not unknown for the best lawyers in the land, the judges of the High Court, to come up with differing answers to legal problems, even to divide four to three. Despite their mutual pretension, judges are as fallible as popes.

An unusually enlightened judicial friend recently reminded me of a decision which underlines the absurdities of which the most gifted legal minds are capable. The facts of this British case were as follows:

Sir Phillip Brocklehurst of Swythamley Hall in Cheshire died in 1975 at the age of 87. A few months before he died he gave a 99-year lease over the shooting rights of his 1600-hectare domain to the owner of a nearby garage, a man with the plain name of John Roberts. Though not a gentleman, John had a gentleman's fondness for shooting.

Sir Phillip had no son and his two daughters by his first marriage were well provided for in their own right. He had only one grandson, of whom the old baronet didn't think much. His estate had some of the best shooting in the country and, deprived of its shooting rights, its value would have been greatly diminished.

In 1972 Lady Brocklehurst, Sir Phillip's second wife, had left him and not returned. Then his old batman, who had looked after him for 40 years, died, leaving him all alone in his big, rambling house. He had met John Roberts about 10 years before he died. For the last two years of his life he had come to rely on John for all sorts of small services.

When Sir Phillip died, his executors challenged the lease on the grounds that it had been secured by John Roberts by the exercise of undue influence on Sir Phillip. The litigation ended up in the Court of Appeal, which upheld the validity of the lease.

But one of the judges dissented and it is his judgment with which we are concerned. In his dissenting judgment, even though he dismissed the allegation of undue influence or indeed of any pressure at all from John Roberts, he found the grant of the lease 'so exceptional and so unreasonable that it cannot stand'.

A reading of his judgment discloses that the judge regarded it as contrary to the natural order that a gentleman, an Eton/Cambridge man and former army officer, should bestow such a gift on the likes of John Roberts, even though, near the end, Sir Phillip had written to him: 'Dear John, you are the best and kindest man friend I have.'

The judge's decision is dripping with almost comical snobbery. It is bad law to boot. Who was the judge? None other than Lord Denning, regarded by many lawyers as the greatest jurist of this century.

Perhaps there are still uses for the jury.

31 July 1991

Siren Call of Adelaide Stirs an Old Man

This year, on our biennial pilgrimage to the Adelaide Festival, the Bride, who is in unchallenged command of such arrangements, decided that our stopover on the first night would be at Mildura. As I am fond of that sparkling, well-tended town I did not demur, despite holding some reservations about her heroic undertaking to drive nearly 1000 kilometres in a day (these days I do not take the wheel myself).

I was assigned the navigation, though my record in that department is patchy. Inevitably, I missed an important turn-off and we fell behind in our self-assigned schedule. On a good road with very little traffic the Bride put her foot down in an attempt to make up the leeway.

At one stage, without either of us noticing it, she hit, as we were informed by the intercepting police officer, 137 km/h according to the radar equipment. It was a fair cop, but the penalty wiped the smile from her face – $250. If she'd been going just a little faster, she was told, the penalty would have been $500 and automatic cancellation of her licence.

Now I would not quarrel with the need to discourage speeding on the roads and the shock certainly had the effect of keeping the Bride grumpily close to the permitted speed for the rest of the journey. But, since human beings are by nature risk-takers, I questioned the wisdom of leaving it to drivers to find out the hard way how drastic are the recently increased penalties for speeding.

Is the purpose to swell the revenues of the State or to make the roads safer? Had I known what the price was I'd certainly have been nagging the needle down.

We got a further unpleasant lesson when we stopped for

a picnic lunch at the town of Narrandera. It is a comely enough place and our lunch spot was a pretty park under a splendid plane tree. While we ate, we watched a lively Aboriginal boy of about three years playing alone on a nearby seesaw. Then a white child of about the same age ran over to the seesaw, and was about to jump on to the seat at the other end, when his mother rushed over and dragged the white child away with a shrill warning: 'You're not going to play with *him*.' What chance is there of inter-racial amity when prejudice is inculcated so early?

Having made it to Mildura, the next day we got lost in McLaren Vale and arrived two hours late at a Writers' Week lunch. Adelaide and environs are the worst-signposted area in the world, and that includes Dublin, which I formerly regarded as the nadir. If you want to get to the Barossa (and who doesn't?) the first mention you'll find of that lovely valley is if and when you've managed to get there.

But the gripes stop at this point. Once in Adelaide you are reminded, especially if you come from a shop-soiled Eden like Sydney, what a civilised city should be like. There is a certain point in the development of a city when quantity has an evil effect on quality. Sydney long since passed that point and I'm afraid it can only get worse.

Adelaide, for fortuitous geographical reasons, has escaped the worst scars of progress. In its case, distance has been not a tyranny but a boon.

There are few high-rise buildings, most of the old Georgian and Victorian architecture survives and the streets are spotlessly clean. They make cars there but the car has not engulfed man; it is a city in which it is still pleasant to walk. Your troubles start only when you want to get out of the city to somewhere else and there is no indication how to get there. Perhaps the authorities believe nobody would ever want to leave.

One of the fringe benefits of an ambience such as Adelaide's is that the annoyances which fret the nerves of the inhabitants of the larger metropolis are so attenuated that the temper of the inhabitants is mild. Cab drivers and shop assistants don't snap at you. Adelaide is our most civil State capital.

It is also the place with the nearest thing to an indigenous aristocracy. On our first night there we saw the Abbey Theatre Company play Sean O'Casey's *Shadow of A Gunman* to this least Irish capital in the country. Adelaide nights are so sure to be hot that visitors and the less affluent locals came in the most informal gear imaginable. But dotted throughout the audience was the occasional unmistakably privileged face beneath which there was a collar and tie or a string of pearls and an over-formal upper-class frock.

Nobody batted an eye when John Bannon, without a minder in sight, slipped into a chair to listen to the scintillating Michael Holroyd read from his biography of Shaw in the Writers' Tent. There, on every day, wit and wisdom abounded. I asked Michael Holroyd if he thought he would have liked Shaw if he had met him in the flesh. 'I have no doubt,' he replied, 'that when he put his mind to it he could be a great charmer. But . . .' and he looked eloquently skyward.

Among the many highlights of an excellent 1990 festival I must mention particularly two outstanding shows of Aboriginal Art, 'Dreamings', at the South Australian Museum, and a marvellous collection of Papunya paintings at the new Tandanya Centre. This superb building is staffed by a bunch of proud, attractive young black people.

What a joy it was to be able to ignore for a while that other tedious festival* I am sworn not to mention. But don't slash your wrists. It will soon be over.

15 March 1990

* The federal election

IF THINGS AIN'T WHAT THEY USED TO BE, THANK YOUR LUCKY STARS

Every now and then there is an outbreak of nostalgia for the good old days. There are always people who get a warm inner glow out of feeling alienated from their time and who hanker after the simpler and nobler life which, they persuade themselves, was the common condition before materialism conquered the civilised world.

The extreme adherents of this view settle at Nimbin, or join the apocalyptic wing of the green movement. While I dislike rampant greed and can't abide yuppies; shed no tears over the downfall of the Bonds and Skases; recognise the threat of the greenhouse effect and agree that some aspects of progress have worsened the human condition; I believe the exaltation of the simple life is a form of romanticism which can be carried too far.

When I think about it, there are many things we didn't have in those good old days and which, for my money, make life more bearable.

Remember when you made a trip to the mountains and on every steep hill you were confronted with cars, bonnets raised, from which steam was pouring? It could happen to anybody. Be grateful for cars that don't overheat.

While we are talking about the much-maligned car, remember that major advance, the windscreen wiper that works, and works at various speeds, and intermittently, if that's what you want. There was a time when you had to resort to smearing the windscreen with a cut potato because your wipers would not do their job.

All men over forty can remember when a shave involved not only lathering your face and scraping off the whiskers, but also dismantling the razor after you'd finished to clean or change the blade. Thank God for disposable razors. Remember, not so long ago, when there was a program on commercial television that you just couldn't afford to miss and you were condemned to watch those awful commercials (weren't they even worse in the good old days)? And the program you wanted to watch almost always started just as you sat down to eat. Now, if you are a member of the 60 per cent or so of Australian households lucky enough to own a video-cassette recorder, you can tape the program, have a leisurely meal, then watch the program and fast-forward the commercials.

In the good old days, making a long-distance phone call meant going through a process of dialling the exchange, waiting for the operator to answer and, when you were finally connected to the number you required, being interrupted by the operator asking, after three minutes, if you wished your time to be extended. If you were not quick, you were disconnected. STD and ISD are among the great boons of modern life.

Instant hot water is an improvement on the tedious old water systems. Remember temperamental gas heaters that ignited with a terrifying bang?

Not only is the 6 o'clock swill at the pub now merely a bad memory, so is the 3 o'clock swill at the bank. And if you were late at the bank on Friday you were cashless for the weekend. Now we can rely on automatic tellers to disgorge cash at any time – or, at least, to tell us we have none left.

Then there is sticky tape, not to mention ballpoint pens. I don't suppose many people remember inkwells. (I must confess that I have recently reverted to a fountain pen, but only because there's a superlative model around today that didn't exist when I previously used one. I can't do a commercial and name it, but anybody who's got one will know which I mean.)

And then there's the daddy (is that sexist?) of them all, those little yellow stickers to mark your place. This has eliminated the dog-ears which marked all those books I devoured before this simple discovery. And students must be grateful for those coloured text-highlighters. And remember those messy carbon copies that were such a pain in the neck for typists? The photocopier (not to mention the computer) put an end to all that.

The choice of cuisines which our multicultural society has made available makes the good old days seem like a hot-dog stand.

Many young people no doubt take all these features of modern life for granted and can't imagine a time when they didn't exist. They are little things, but for the most of us life is an aggregation of trivia.

In case I should be accused of being blinded by progress, let me confess that I do not regard all of its features with unalloyed joy. For example, I'm unimpressed when the automatic teller swallows my card and refuses to disgorge it, or closes as I arrive.

Maybe I just lack hand-eye co-ordination but I get a wrong number on at least one in three calls I make on a push-button phone.

Muzak while you are on hold does not improve the temper, nor do car phones and the types who use them.

Things like screws and batteries that are so packaged that you can hardly get at them do nothing good to my blood pressure.

I can't recall any expressions of the past quite so inane as 'no worries', or 'have a nice day'.

I need to take lessons in how to unravel a newspaper that comes in plastic wrap.

I'm constitutionally incapable of coping with complex electronic equipment, such as oven-timers (does anyone use them?) My mail suggests I am far from being alone in this.

In the good old days, it seems to me, it didn't rain all the time in summer – which began in November not January – and winters were really winters.

And how did ice-creams get to cost $1.50?

Life gets better in some ways, worse in others. But for most of us whose memories go back far enough, the good old days are a fond dream of a state that never existed.

15 February 1990

ABORIGINAL IMAGES IN PERSPECTIVE

A recent visitor to our house was a forty-year-old Aboriginal man who has spent a total of sixteen years in jail and who was released a few months ago after his latest stretch.

His crimes have been serious, including armed robbery. I made his acquaintance in an unusual way. A couple of years ago a young man, the son of old and highly respectable friends of my own vintage, was released from jail. He, too, had drifted into a life of crime to feed his heroin habit. In jail he had met the Aboriginal man, whom I'll call John for convenience, and they became close friends.

On discharge, my old friends' son got in touch with me and told me John, who was still in jail, would be pleased to get a letter from me. We became correspondents and I was immediately impressed by his intelligence and character. I asked him to call on me when the parole he was expecting eventuated. Hence his recent visit.

What would the average white Australian, reared on the historical, media-fostered stereotype of an Aborigine (let alone a hardened criminal, as John readily admitted himself to have been), expect such a man to be like?

He turned out to be a handsome, fit, articulate man who has steadfastly eschewed drugs and who drinks only occasionally. While in jail he applied for and, on release, got a counselling job in the Aboriginal Welfare Service and is now stationed in a large, western town. We talked for three hours and I found him well-informed, insightful about himself, lacking in bitterness or self-pity. He is determined to use the rest of his life productively and to make up for the years he has wasted during his anti-social past. He is a man of formidable dignity.

The federal Minister for Aboriginal Affairs, Robert Tickner, remarked recently that millions of Australian people have never met an Aborigine. They may have seen them through the windows of their cars as they pass through towns or suburbs where they live, but otherwise they rely for their images of Australian blacks on media headlines (they rarely bother themselves with the details underneath) and on TV pictures of selected aspects of the way some Aborigines live. But for most whites, to meet Aborigines in person is a comparatively rare event.

My view was similarly limited until I spent almost a year on a radar station on Bathurst Island during the war. This is the traditional home of the Tiwi tribe and it was my first opportunity to get to know Aborigines as human beings rather than the stereotyped image to which I had been conditioned. I claim no marks for the quite adventitious cure which I underwent of the inherited white prejudice against Aborigines, but fortunately that experience killed the virus for the rest of my life.

Unhappily, it survives and flourishes in circles where it can do the most damage, for example, among the police. This is one of the conclusions which was highlighted by the findings of the Royal Commission into Aboriginal Deaths in Custody. I had personal experience of this prejudice when a local policeman called to investigate a burglary at our house. In the course of the interview he casually dropped the word 'coon' into his conversation. What was particularly shocking was his obvious assumption that the word could not be offensive to fellow whites.

The widespread negative view of Aborigines was referred to by Mr Tickner in a recent address to the Australian Centre for Independent Journalism. We are accustomed to ample reporting of events showing Aborigines in a bad light. Another speaker at the same meeting, Irene Moss, the Race Discrimination Commissioner, pointed out this may be largely attributed to the old media adage that bad news is good news and good news is no news.

The good news about which Mr Tickner was talking was the historic cross-party support which had just been given in federal parliament to a process of reconciliation between Aboriginal and non-Aboriginal people to operate until the centenary of federation in 2001. A major part of that process will be a campaign to create a much greater awareness of Aboriginal issues in the wider community.

In this process there is a leading role for the media, which must lift its form on previous performances. For example, without in any way playing down the problem of alcoholism among Aborigines, the media might convey the news to the white population that the percentage of Aborigines who drink is smaller than that of the non-Aboriginal community who drink.

Or, instead of portraying Redfern as a ghetto of drunken no-hopers, some attention might be given to the program under which Aborigines in the area voluntarily forgo their right to unemployment benefits, such benefits are pooled and the people work on community projects, including a face-lift for Redfern's more dilapidated houses.

And the prominent columnist in a leading newspaper who recently poured scorn and derision on Aboriginal spiritual beliefs might be told by his editor that, in a community which prides itself on its religious tolerance, such outpourings of sectarian bile are just as distasteful as when they are directed at Catholics, Jews or Muslims.

24 July 1991

CAUTION, BIG OBJECTS ON THE ROAD

Travelling north provides even more lessons than are to be derived from David Williamson's entertaining play of the same name.

When the Bride and I recently succumbed to one of our periodic attacks of wanderlust and headed in that direction, we made a discovery which deserves to be the subject of a PhD thesis: the warmer the climate, the greater the human fixation on gigantism.

It starts at Coffs Harbour with the Big Banana, an outsize replica of that fruit, which adorns (if that is the right word) a large plantation covering the side of a sizeable mountain. As one proceeds north, each region's notable feature appears in similar aggrandised form, thus the Big Oyster, the Big Prawn and the Big Fish.

After having been exposed to those samples of the fad, followed by the Big Pineapple, the Big Apple (and even the Big Bottle), I developed a craving for a small grape. The last straw was a huge plastic representation of a Big Pelican, positioned so as to direct the eye at what only the blind could miss – a lake on which real specimens of that stately bird disport themselves.

The scenery remains obstinately beautiful despite the creeping 'Floridation' (not to be confused with fluoridation, but signifying the practice of taking hold of a paradise and attempting to turn it into an approximation of Miami) of the landscape. Apart from this, a lot of entertainment is to be had from the signs along the roadway.

My favourite was 'Half Dead Chook $3.95'. Were customers being offered a whole but not completely extinct chicken for the stated price? Guaranteed freshness might be the message, just as diners are enticed to choose a live lobster for their meal from a restaurant fish tank. Or were we dealing with a thoroughly dead bird of which we might have half for $3.95? Then why mention 'dead'? If only half was being offered, was not prior death to be presumed?

Then there was the constantly recurring warning 'Falling Rocks. Don't Stop'. Did that mean that if a falling boulder descended on the roof of your car, you were expected to be sufficiently indestructible and suffused with civic duty to keep going in order to avoid blocking the traffic? Or, that if you pressed resolutely on when rocks started to fall, you would have a better chance of the rocks missing you? I recalled the old song *Running Between the Raindrops*. On any interpretation, it seemed that the inevitability of rocks falling was accepted by the authorities, that they did not propose to do anything about it, and that, if anything happened to motorists as a result of this incurable phenomenon, they would be held accountable.

Then there are the signs on the cars themselves, which are, of course, not peculiar to the journey in question. I have often wondered whether the announcement 'Baby on Board' was merely an advertisement of procreational achievement, or was intended to deter drivers from an otherwise uncontrollable urge to run into the car in front of them. I would have thought self-preservation was a sufficient deterrent, without adding the threat of infanticide.

In the same category is the 'Caution Horses' sign on the floats being drawn by drivers anxious for the safety of their valuable freight. Does that suggest that a thoroughbred horse, by instinct resistant to being passed, will bite any would-be passers? They don't do it on the racetrack. Why on the road? The only people who don't like horses are bankrupt punters but even they are likely to place their own physical survival ahead of revenge on the species that has caused their ruin.

Most of the towns along the way are steadily succumbing to the Miami syndrome. One featured, cheek by jowl, a Pizza Hut, a Kentucky Fried Chicken and a golden-arched McDonald's – a triptych of vulgarity.

By now, alert readers will have guessed we are over the State line and in territory where the Miles Franklin award was reported by the media as having been awarded to BRISBANE-BORN David Malouf.

Bearing in mind that southerners can expect no quarter from the authorities, the Bride drove virtuously within the limit and stuck to the left lane. We were on the main road into Brisbane, the Bruce Highway, and we soon noticed that cars with Queensland number-plates were hurtling past on our right at speeds up to 140 km/h. After a while, an intrepid NSW driver, evidently acting on the when-in-Rome principle, pulled over to the right lane and joined the speedsters. The next we saw of him was at the side of the road alongside a cop with book and pen at the ready.

Don't get me wrong. This is not a hymn of hatred against Queensland, which, despite humanity's worst endeavours, remains probably the best naturally endowed region of this country. We dined one full-moon night with friends from whose veranda you can almost touch the bizarrely beautiful Glass House Mountains. And despite some architectural extravaganzas on its shores, the sea at Noosa still shimmers as it did when it was a quiet fishing village.

If I may adapt the old description of the Crimean resort of Yalta, Queensland is a place where every natural prospect pleases but most of the development is vile.

3 July 1991

CHARMED LIVES, ALL NINE OF THEM

A few days ago I came upon the Bride chortling over the morning paper. When I inquired about the source of her mirth, she replied: 'When you've finished with all that turgid political guff in the first section of the paper, just cast your eyes over this.'

'This' turned out to be a piece in the Good Living section of this paper, entitled 'Claws'. It was a light-hearted tribute to the charms of the cat and contained some interesting statistics, such as the fact that there are 2.8 million cats in Australia, spread over more than a third of all households.

Now the Bride is what you might call a felophile from way back while I am a comparatively recent convert. And, like all converts, I am more of a zealot than those born to a faith.

You know all those former non-believers or lukewarm

Anglicans who suddenly see a blinding light and from then on act as though they had invented Catholicism.

So, after doing my own share of chuckling, I bridled at the following remark on the limitations of feline endowment: 'On a cerebral development chart, a cat falls somewhere between a gerbil and a marmoset.'

Think of that: your moggy sandwiched between a mouse-like desert rodent and a small tropical monkey.

I had, of course, heard of the marmoset, but gerbil was a new one on me. I went looking for further and better particulars in my bible, *The Shorter Oxford English Dictionary*, where I had to be content with: 'Gerbile (also Gerbil): Any animal belonging to the *genus Gerbillus*.' In any event, I realised that a slur was being cast on the intellectual capacity of our Grace, so named after the department store of her provenance.

'Ridiculous,' I expostulated. 'What about the way Grace discovered that warm mat in the bathroom? Doesn't that show brains?'

(In preparation for the Siberian winter of the Blue Mountains, we had recently installed a heating system which, inter alia, warms the bathroom floor. In discovering this innovation Grace, whose regular matutinal habit had been to leap on to our bed with a loud announcement of her presence, is now to be found in the morning on a mat on the bathroom floor.)

'That's not brains,' was the Bride's riposte. 'That's the great cat instinct for looking after number one.'

I did not surrender lightly, pointing out that, according to the currently popular ethos, looking after number one was esteemed as the primary manifestation of genius. 'Anyhow,' I tried as a last-ditch argument, 'how many people do you know who keep a gerbil or a marmoset?'

But that really had nothing to do with the subject of our dissension and the Bride, who has a stronger grip on logic than I have, pointed out that I was confusing charm with intellect.

Surely cats, whose skills are confined to catching animals smaller than themselves (and the more pampered they are, the more even that skill becomes blunted) are the ultimate illustrations of the power of charm in getting by in this world!

Bob Hawke has proclaimed as a national goal that, instead of being content to be a lucky country, we should aspire to be a clever country.

I have no quarrel with the proposition that we could all benefit from an increased cerebral input into all spheres of human endeavour, not excluding the arena where the Prime Minister earns his living.

But if I were assembling a guest-list for a convivial lunch I would baulk at a suggestion that the gathering should be confined to those who have a reputation, whether deserved or not, for being clever.

Just think of the motley crew who would rate a guernsey according to the fashionable view of cleverness: John Elliott, Harry Miller, Kerry Packer, Bronwyn Bishop, Sam Chisholm, Leonie Kramer, Richard Carleton, John Laws and many highly publicised medicos and lawyers.

By the time the entrees had been served, wouldn't most of us non-geniuses be looking for the exit door?

So what if cats are not clever? The people characterised in this society as being clever are so frequently unlovable – even repulsive – that cleverness does not rate at the top of my list of desirable characteristics.

At least, not among the people I want to know.

Now I would not like it to be thought that I am singing a psalm of praise to stupidity. It could be argued that the most precious natural resource of any society is its stock of brainy people.

The benefits conferred on everybody by the efforts of the exceptionally talented are obvious.

The best people of more than ordinary endowment – in practical inventiveness, in literature, science, the arts, even in politics – are those whose brilliance is tempered by humanity, sensitivity, commonsense.

But some of the greatest geniuses of history have, sadly, been pretty objectionable. I certainly wouldn't have wanted to know Tolstoy or George Bernard Shaw, or Richard Wagner.

So, let's be thankful for what we get from clever people but let's also enjoy what the not-so-clever have to offer.

Like cats.

4 June 1990

A GERIATRIC SACRIFICE TO THE ELECTRONIC AGE

I paid a visit to the house of friends who had been away for five years. 'And how's little Peter?' I asked my hostess after the initial pleasantries. 'Wait and see,' she replied with an implied caution in her voice.

The day before I had had a visit from my grown-up daughter who, in the course of conversation, had recalled 'those awful dinner parties you used to have when I had to pass the olives around and cop that "my, how you've grown" routine'. So at least I was forewarned not to try that one on little Peter, who had been nine when I last saw him.

Just as well. Little Peter, now taller than me, was seated at his computer. He threw me a friendly but casual "Hi" and kept punching away at that keyboard with the screen in front. I experienced that familiar fossil-feeling which comes over geriatric technological illiterates in the presence of the young initiates of the electronic age.

I can just imagine little Peter, if he were to come upon me in the act of writing this column, reporting to his parents: 'You know that old guy who was here the other day? He uses a fountain pen!'

In this field I am a museum-piece. Manually dexterous I am not. In fact, when it comes to anything practical, let alone mechanical, my natural aptitude and acquired skills are fully extended coping with a tin opener.

This is a humiliating era for people like me. If I were not so well into the sere and yellow I'd feel like doing something about it, but I'm probably beyond cure.

Take the VCR. I am totally ignorant of how to turn it on. Actually getting it to play a tape, let alone setting it to record something would be, for me, a feat on a par with mastering the theory of relativity. In fact, the only way I can distinguish it from the stereo system is that the video is closer to the television. I'm comforted by my observations that many otherwise competent people get their kids to program these mysterious machines for them. It helps to know you are not the only technological nincompoop.

About 20 years ago, when I was a bit more mobile, I was persuaded that I might derive both pleasure and a postponement of physical decay if I took up riding a bike in lovely nearby Centennial Park. So I bought an expensive bike – though not in the class of the sort that Leo Schofield rides, which cannot cost much less than a Porsche.

I soon had to give up this new-found joy. Remember Lyndon Johnson's coarse remark about Gerald Ford not being able to chew gum and fart at the same time? Well, I ran into a tree because I couldn't steer and change gears at the same time.

For an inordinately long time after they had won general acceptance, I resisted automatic bank tellers. I was ultimately shamed into falling in line with the multitude by the derision of my long-suffering wife, upon whom I have to rely when I can't get the television to work because I have inadvertently disconnected the aerial and can't find the hole into which it fits. 'Any moron can use an automatic bank-teller,' she scoffed.

One day she picked a remote and apparently little-used automatic teller machine to give me a lesson. By the time I had pressed all the wrong buttons and managed to retrieve the card, a lengthy queue had formed. Undaunted, I took to hovering around the machines until I was convinced that some of the people inserting their cards and making a few quick movements did not look quite like Einsteins. Finally I became a user.

Recently, I was looking through an album of photographs taken on one of our forays into unfamiliar places. There was one of my wife standing in front of an old outback pub with its name 'Ilverton' emblazoned near its roof.

My camera skills had not been sufficient to get the full name into the picture: it was the famous Silverton pub, near Broken Hill, which is so picturesque and 'authentic' that films have been made there.

I have done worse, including a shot of the Great Wall of China running vertically instead of horizontally.

To compensate for being so under-equipped for modern living I have certain purely decorative skills which predate the electronic revolution. There's one thing I can do which I bet little Peter can't: I can tie a bow tie.

Having been something of a fop in my day, I acquired, early in my sartorial conditioning, a towering contempt for the 'stinker'. This, in the lexicon of the dude, is the name for the pre-tied sort that you merely slip under your collar and fasten at the back. The stinker looks much neater but there's the rub. That look of throwaway nonchalance which is the aim of all fops and which takes so much time and trouble to achieve can only be managed with a careful/careless bow of your own tying.

There's an art to it, but once you've mastered it you can do it in your sleep. It's a skill of which I'm inordinately proud.

After all, any moron can operate a VCR.

17 August 1989

POLITICAL FOOTBALL AND THE POPULARITY STAKES

In cynical Sydney, a politician who kisses babies in public does not ordinarily persuade voters that he is fond of children. Conversely, in Melbourne, a politician who does *not* support a football team is suspected of abnormal tendencies. So universal is football piety down there that the public is prepared to make an exception to the general rule that anything a politician does in public can have only one purpose: to attract votes.

However, there were some mystified comments, both in Melbourne and Sydney, when our Treasurer, who has hitherto been hooked on clocks but cold on sport, suddenly emerged as an enthusiast for the MELBOURNE brand of football which is mostly despised in the States where Rugby League is king.

A document which fell off the back of a truck and landed in your columnist's lap may help to throw some light on what, from a political point of view, may appear a trifle aberrant.

I can't vouch for its accuracy. It may even be a deliberate piece of misinformation planted perhaps by some outraged Rugby League fanatic. But since it is not defamatory and may even be true, I offer it for what it is worth. It purports to be a transcript of a meeting attended by Paul Keating (PK), an unidentified minder (M) and a PR person. To protect the latter's anonymity I will refer to him merely as JS. So here goes:

PK: What do you blokes think you're paid for? You know that old Jellyback will bow out early next year and I'll be the top dog. That's the easy part, as Barrie Unsworth found out. But winning an election is harder. To do that, they tell me, you have to be liked. It was hard for anybody to like Bazza and I've picked up a few vibes that those clowns out there are not all that crazy about me.

M: Well Minister, old Jell . . . – sorry, the PM – always had the right formula: to be like the rest of the mob. Remember when Bondy – sorry, that reckless entrepreneur, Alan Bond – took the Cup off the Yanks? Hawkie was right in the middle of the celebrations.

He's always at the races, or a cricket match (especially against the Poms) or a footy match, or golf (when Greg Norman is proving Aussies are as good as anyone and probably better).

And, if I may say so without disrespect, all they hear about you when you are not putting the boot into them is hanging around Bill Bradshaw's shop in Woollahra perving on some old clock. That makes you look like some sort of a poof or something.

PK: Watch your tongue, sleazebag! What about you, Mr PR genius? Have you got any ideas to justify the zillions we pay you?

JS: Yes, old mate. You have to pick yourself a football team and APPEAR to be wrapped in it. It can get pretty boring but, let's face it, you wouldn't be taking on the PM's job if you couldn't take a bit of boredom.

PK: Well, I suppose Canterbury-Bankstown is the natural team for me to pick. I grew up there, I represent the district, I own a house there, I even visit the place a couple of times a year.

JS: Wrong. In the first place, Canterbury-Bankstown is buried down in the middle of the premiership ladder. Not even the Pope would be able to pray them into the first five this year.

You don't want to be associated with a loser in your first year as a fan. Besides, you've got to think of energy-effectiveness. If you've got to drag yourself to a match every

Saturday do it where you and the party most need to lift your game: Victoria.

PK: What? Put up with (expletive deleted) aerial ping-pong every week!

M: JS is right, boss. We'd be trailing behind the Trotskyists down there at the moment. You've got to do something about Victoria or it's back to Elizabeth Bay for you after the election.

PK: Then what team do I pick down there? All I know about Melbourne football is that even though Elliott's grip on Fosters may be slipping, he still owns Carlton Football Club.

JS: I've been giving the matter some thought. Essendon and Collingwood are sharing the lead at the moment and the good money says one of them should win this year. But it would be a bad omen to pick Essendon. That's Peacock's team and look where backing them got him! So, logically, it's got to be Collingwood. You'll have to learn to scream: Carna Pies.

PK: What's that mean?

JS: Come on Magpies. Their colours are black and white, see.

PK: OK. Spread the word that I've seen the light and I'll be at next Saturday's game. Don't say anything about the VIP jet. The mugs out there won't understand that I can't afford more than three hours away from the Budget. I don't suppose it would look right if I were dropped in the middle of the ground from an Army helicopter?

M: I'll sound out Bobby Ray about that, but I doubt that he'd cop it. I know Kim wouldn't have when he was Minister for Defence. Had to tighten the belt to pay for those submarines. I'll get back to you. [Document ends.]

As I said, I wouldn't go to the barricades over the authenticity of that document, but it does have that ring of statesmanship that we have come to associate with our Treasurer.

But if those sleazebags of the Opposition have got their figures right and the VIP jet to Paul's first game cost the taxpayers a cool $4280, he may find it wise to change his advisers on how to get popular.

If you set out to woo the public it's not very smart to start off by picking their pockets.

24 July 1990

SENTENCING POLICY AND LIFETIMES OF REGRET

There are always elements in society which find an answer to all social problems in governments 'getting tougher' - on unions, on junkies, on criminals, and less frequently on tax dodgers. There is probably some reaction to pressure of that kind in NSW Attorney General John Dowd's decision that in future a sentence of life imprisonment will mean just what it says.

Today everyone knows, including the judge and the person sentenced, that he/she will rarely serve a full life term and will generally serve much less. Under the law as it stands, the life sentence for murder is mandatory unless there are mitigating circumstances in the commission of the crime. But the fate of the person sentenced is not decided for ever at the moment of sentence. His/her conduct after sentence, and exceptional circumstances such as illness, are relevant to the term which will actually be served.

Sometimes, as in the case of a particularly gruesome crime, such as the Anita Cobby murder, a judge will add a recommendation that convicted persons should never be released. But even such a recommendation has no binding effect. Under the proposed change in the law, the judge will have unfettered discretion to impose any sentence for murder, up to a life sentence, and know the full term will be served. This is a sensible recognition that the degrees of culpability for murder may vary enormously.

The real change proposed is that a sentence of life

imprisonment should no longer be tampered with, as at present. In my view, it is a retrograde step to repose in one person, no matter how wise and learned, the power to put an end to another person's right to freedom, forever, and with no regard to the conduct of that person subsequent to sentence.

This entire philosophical debate, which is as old as humankind, ultimately rests on the question: What is the social purpose of punishment for crime?

I think I can understand the feelings of someone who has lost a dear one through the wanton act and can imagine that my own initial reaction might be similar. But I don't believe murder justifies a vengeful response from society and I hope that would be my final opinion after the initial shock.

The most pragmatic justification for severe punishment of crime is deterrent. But history suggests that this often collides with other, stronger human tendencies such as greed, lust, anger or just plain willingness to take the odds against being caught. This is not an argument against any form of social retribution, rather a warning of its limitations.

The most impressive justification for severe punishment is the protection of society from people with a proved uncontrollable impulse to violence. Such people undoubtedly exist, but the statistics on recidivist murder suggest they are relatively rare.

The overwhelming majority of lawbreakers are redeemable by methods other than long periods of incarceration; and a policy of rehabilitation rather than draconian punishment, despite its failures, is not only more humane but more socially productive.

But the most practical objection I have to the Dowd proposal is that it will not achieve its avowed objective of bringing more certainty into the process of punishment for murder.

It is well known among lawyers that there is a wide divergence of attitudes toward the punishment, not only for murder but for most crimes, among the judiciary. Every lawyer practising in the criminal field can tell you which judges would react to the enlargement of their punitive powers by welcoming the opportunity to put offenders away forever and which (the majority, I believe) would be loath to impose a sentence of permanent imprisonment.

Judge-shopping, contrived excuses for postponement, deliberate abortion of trials in the hope of getting a more lenient judge next time would further aggravate the logjams in our already malfunctioning system of justice.

Even more seriously, the knowledge that a conviction for murder may result in permanent incarceration, so unlikely under the law as it stands, would put a new, powerful weapon in the hands of the prosecution to persuade the accused to plead guilty to the lesser charge of manslaughter, so relieving the Crown of the task of proving it.

I believe John Dowd is a compassionate man, and suggest he should take another look at his proposal.

4 August 1989

THE STING IS WORSE THAN THE BARK

I must be one of the few Australians who have never seen the soapie *Neighbours*. For that omission I felt a mite unpatriotic on an occasion a couple of years ago when we were touring Ireland. At one point we strayed briefly into Ulster and, at a border town on our way back into the Republic, we were stopped at a checkpoint and our passports were inspected.

After satisfying himself we were not terrorists, the young English soldier who had quizzed us said: 'Australian, eh? Do you come from Melbourne?' Why, we asked, was he interested in Melbourne? 'That's where they make *Neighbours*,' he replied. He never missed an episode.

Recently I had occasion to regret this cultural oversight of mine. Surely a series which seems to have been running since the birth of television and has even won English fans must, if only in a desperate search for a new idea, have touched on a question of neighbourliness on which I would welcome some advice: what is the best way to behave towards neighbours with whom your relations are friendly or at least neutral, when you are being driven mad by one or more of their pets? The question does not arise if you already hate each other's guts. If you've reached the stage of fisticuffs, parliamentary insults or injunctions, one more brawl will make no difference.

But if you want to stay on good terms with the neighbours, the problem is more difficult. Friends of ours were ultimately driven to sell their house to escape a couple of dogs which yapped incessantly from the moment their owners went out until the moment they returned. The dogs' owners who, of course, were never similarly troubled by their little angels, took umbrage at our friends' mild complaint and relations soured to the point where someone had to go.

These same friends, who now live in a salubrious street and who keep a cherished old dog who is too feeble to bark, felt somewhat put-upon recently when a roneoed copy of a handwritten notice was dropped in their letter-box. If I may quote the preface to the old television series, *The Naked City*, only the names have been changed to protect the innocent:

HOMER AND VIRGIL STREETS
(between Pound and Dollar Streets)
A few hours out of a typical weekend:

Saturday, May 4

4-ish to 6-ish pm	Large barking dog – constant
6-ish to 8-ish pm	Small yapping dog – constant

Sunday, May 5

4 am to 5 am	Small yapping dog – infuriating
6.30 to 7.30 am	Large barking dog

HAVE A GOOD WEEKEND!

Our friends' indignation at being falsely accused of unneighbourly conduct abated on their discovery that all their neighbours had received the circular – evidently a rather cunning ploy to enlist the support of the innocent as well as to shame the guilty.

But the real sting was on the reverse side of the notice, which carried a copy of a report which recently appeared in this paper under the byline of Cathy Johnson.

It drew attention to the virtuoso skill of one Sylvia Wilson who, with her husband Danny, runs a firm which specialises in taking the bark out of dogs. Sylvia simply approaches the noisy animal and out-barks it. She can evidently silence even a doberman with this trick – permanently, after a two-hour session of therapy.

Ms Johnson also wrote that from 1 July, under a recent amendment to the law, owners of persistently barking dogs who, after a prior warning, have been served with a bark-abatement notice, may get an on-the-spot fine of $200, without the opportunity to contest the charge in court.

If our letter writer was not simply an agent for Sylvia and Danny, he or she was at least an unconscious promoter of good old-fashioned capitalist initiative in these days of scarce job opportunities. Unless Sylvia and Danny can move quickly to tie up the market (and surely there's only so much barking any human being can do in a day) the really bright boys and girls will grab the ball those two have kicked onto the level playing field and run with it.

Our approach to this problem has hardly been an example of lateral thinking. It's a waste of time trying to change the habits of human beings. Pet therapy is the way to go.

So, in addition to macro- and micro- we can now also have cano-reform. And for those old-fashioned socialists who still think there's a role for government in human affairs, the power to exact fines can provide the stimulus to entrepreneurs to hone and market their product. There's even room for a bit of graft, as in any well-run polity. As in the tow-truck rort, an unscrupulous pet therapist might work in cahoots with noise abatement officers who, for a bit of income-enhancement, could refer them to potential customers.

Bark-modifying training schools will soon spring up all over the suburbs. Bark-therapists will attain the status of auditors, physicians, marriage counsellors. Unemployed children fresh from the best schools will queue up for training in this new calling.

Soon there will be specialists within the specialty, such as therapists who can out-honk a goose. After all, every profession needs its QCs.

29 May 1991

COME AND SEE US SOME (OTHER) TIME

It was one of those benign mountain days. The Bride and I decided to stroll down to the local pub for lunch. It is an excellent hostelry with a pleasant proprietor, a good chef and a wide range of beers and wines.

We do this every now and then. Although the pub is always well patronised, we can usually count on getting one of our favourite tables on an enclosed verandah with a view across the picturesque railway station, the highway and our little village to distant foothills. Here we quaff and dine modestly but well.

This day a large tourist bus standing in the pub grounds caused us some uneasiness. Sure enough, almost every table was occupied, mostly by men and women of my own vintage, that is, getting on a bit. The men were jockey-capped and garishly T-shirted in that unmistakably American gesture of defiance to the ageing process; the women were pants-suited and blue-rinsed. All wore what the Bride told me were Reeboks. Their level of conversation was several decibels higher than that of the regulars.

We had to settle for a non-verandah table, and caught the proprietor's eye. We complimented him on being so busy, and he raised his eyes heavenwards. 'There's not much cop in it for me,' he said. 'They're all drinking iced water.' For some reason which has always escaped me, few Americans seem to have realised that drink and food get along well together.

The trouble about living in a beautiful part of the world is that you can count on the word getting out to others besides yourself, and the word has certainly got around about the Blue Mountains. The boost to trade has delighted the local shopkeepers, and the modern god Tourism is enthusiastically enshrined here as elsewhere.

It would be curmudgeonly to begrudge others the aesthetic feasts which we enjoy, and, of course, I would not be advertising them if I did not accept the inevitability of this process. But experience has taught me there is a price to be paid for living amid beauty.

Many years ago, I 'discovered' Noosa on Queensland's Sunshine Coast – then a delicious little village with fashionable shops, good eating places, a magical beach and, for good measure, a walk around the cliffs through a carefully protected national park from which cars were excluded. All this added up to a feast for jaded city dwellers.

A few years later I returned to find Noosa had been discovered by the white-shoe brigade. Developers had plans for buildings which would overshadow the beach, and the place was acquiring the ambience of Surfers Paradise. I am old enough to remember when even that modern gem of vulgarity was fit for human habitation. *Sic transit.*

The most grievous price that can be paid by permanent residents in a tourist mecca is a steady deterioration in the manners of those who service the tourists.

The ultimate example of this unfortunate downside of beautiful places is Paris. It never disappoints the eye, but only the most long-suffering saint can emerge without experiencing an almost overpowering urge to strangle a few Parisians.

On a visit some time during the 1960s my wife and I had occasion to avail ourselves of the services of the international travel firm of Thomas Cook and Sons. Its very *raison d'être* was to provide service and advice to travellers, many of whom, by definition, could not be expected to understand French.

We wanted to make some plane bookings and, though we were both proficient enough in French to read a book or a newspaper in that language, we were too intimidated by Parisians' linguistic snobbery (they even pretend not to understand French provincials) to try to speak the language to the snooty-looking clerk behind the counter.

After we had vainly tried to get our message across in English we gave up and did our stumbling best in French. He listened for a while superciliously, and then burst into flawless English. Having put us in our place, he was prepared to do business with us.

Another time we presented ourselves, after a hair-raising taxi ride, at a restaurant near the Gare du Nord which had been highly touted to us. As we opened the door we saw it was chock-a-block.

Before we could even turn to leave, the proprietress swooped on us and pushed us into the street, almost under the wheels of passing cars, which, I felt sure, were doing their best to run us down.

I have no doubt there are charming and polite Parisians, but they must hide from tourists.

However, I think I have come to understand the cause of Parisian irascibility, at least at the height of the tourist season. Paris is, after all, *their* city.

Much of its prosperity, of course, is due to the tourist industry. But when tourists clutter their beautiful streets, elbow them out of their favourite restaurants, clog their theatres and museums, is it any wonder that they get cranky?

Thankfully, the Blue Mountains has so far managed to keep

the friendly, courteous service characteristic of Australia outside the major cities. I hope it never becomes Parisianised – or, for that matter, Sydneyfied.

21 November 1990

I LOVE MUM AND MOZART

The Victorian town of Bright snuggles in its greenery at the foot of Mount Buffalo. In the course of our recent meanderings in the Australian alpine region, the Bride and I paused there one day and were sipping our cappuccinos at an open-air cafe when a possibly freakish event befell us.

I noticed a man coming in our direction who somehow managed to combine in his person an air of carefree relaxation with a certain gravitas. He was about fifty and his dress could not have been more casual – runners, jeans and a blue singlet. But his slightly stern, erect bearing might have been that of a judge, in holiday mode but refraining from letting his hair right down.

As he drew abreast and passed our table, the ambiguity of his aspect took on a touch almost of the bizarre. On his upper left arm there was a largish tattoo and I would have been prepared to swear an affidavit there and then that it was a faithful representation of a certain W. A. Mozart.

As soon as he was out of earshot, I elbowed the Bride, whose attention had been elsewhere, and spluttered (almost hysterically, she later said): 'That man has a tattoo of Mozart on his arm.'

Although the singlet lent some plausibility to the presence of a tattoo, her reaction was that I was slightly addled by the hot sun: in general, people who went in for tattoos could be relied on never to have heard of old Wolfgang Amadeus, let alone to award him such a prominent position on the limited space of their body surface.

Half, but only half, convinced that I must have been hallucinating, and not being prepared to go to the barricades over such a trifle, I accepted her dismissal of my folly. However, on returning to our home base a few days later, I was reminded by several articles in the papers that 1991 had been designated as the Year of Mozart, in recognition of its being the bicentennial year of the great man's death in 1791. Perhaps, after all, that explained what I thought I had seen in Bright.

But I could not budge the Bride from her disbelief. Rising to the challenge, I set about mounting an argument like a barrister with a hopeless brief of which he is determined to make the most.

Yes, I conceded, the exponential growth of the craze to be tattooed on almost any (and preferably every) part of the body, which had made it such a flourishing industry in recent years, had hardly touched the culture vultures. Bikies and other sociological subgroups were much more likely than aesthetes to have their skin defaced by a practice which originated, so the archeologists assured us, during the Palaeolithic age, and which is generally associated with primitive man.

Who would want to profane the memory of the divine Mozart by placing him in the company of indelibly stained perforations of snakes and arrowed hearts and I Love Jennys?

But that, I argued, warming to my brief, was a simplistic view of the matter. Perhaps the singleted man of Bright was one of those courageous souls prepared to swim against the tide of contumely heaped by the cognoscenti on the tattooed multitude.

Could he, perhaps, surveying the mounting mass of needled flesh that meets our gaze every day in the cities of this land, have decided: if you can't beat them, join them? If the trend, as one may be forgiven for concluding, is to become almost universal, why cede the field to the philistines? Why not detrivialise the tattoo by turning it into an art form, celebrating the cultural heroes of yesterday and today? Such a crusade would also provide an indirect subsidy to the arts by fostering a new brand of artist, the Rembrandts of the needle.

It might also introduce a new frisson into a field of human activity where the innovative is always welcome, namely sex, by adding a new dimension to getting your gear off. Getting to know one another might be fraught with such stimulating surprises as finding Tolstoy staring at you from above a navel or J. S. Bach beaming from a buttock.

At the end of my endeavours I decided that I would hate to be a barrister pleading a cause with the Bride on the jury. She told me she would consider giving her blessing to such a crusade if I would set an example by having a tattoo of those two old scrappers, Sidney Nolan and Patrick White, one on the left and one on the right thigh just below the shorts line. I'm thinking it over.

13 February 1991

WHY JAMES INSTEAD OF JASON?

'Tiffany, stop picking on Troy.' On a steamy day outside our local supermarket I heard a harassed mum utter this shrill reproof to her seven-ish daughter, who, in the manner of bored kids, especially when their parents are frazzled, was teasing a younger sibling.

Earlier this month, this paper announced on its front page that the most popular names of 1990, as published in the *Herald*'s birth notices, were Jessica and James. On an inside page was a list of the 25 most popular male and female names, and the 20 most popular second names. There were no Tiffanys or Troys in those lists.

Judging from the names I hear most commonly tossed

around in public places, I can only conclude that there are a lot of parents who are not letting the world know per medium of the *SMH* birth notices the fancy names with which they are sending their progeny forth to face the world.

I suppose it is a particularly January-ish foible to indulge oneself in more than a moment's attention to the question of names, especially with war raging, the ever-present threat of bushfires and the record number of bankruptcies. However, while catastrophes, horrible and recurrent as they are, eventually go away, we are stuck with our names for life (unless we become movie stars and those who take over our lives give us a new monicker).

A phenomenon of our times is that today people actually get called by the names they were given. Back in the distant days of my childhood, if you were named John or Richard or Robert or James or William, it was taken for granted that nobody would ever call you anything but Jack, Dick, Bob, Jim or Bill. Elizabeth infallibly became Betty; Margaret – inexplicably – Peggy.

It would have been considered 'pansy' to be called by the name your parents had selected for you. The only times my mother called me James were when she was annoyed with me, obliquely confirming the pejorative aura attached to your formal name.

(I can't decide whether it is a mark of distinction or the commonplace that my own name heads the list. In the British list, based on birth announcements in the *Times*, it also came top of the list for the 27th consecutive year. But sharp-eyed readers might have noticed that whereas my byline started off as James McClelland, my editors ultimately changed it to Jim. Evidently they couldn't take seriously a name by which nobody ever addressed me.)

The names parents select for their children tell us a lot about their social attitudes. The *SMH* and *Times* lists are a mark of the traditionalism of those who use their columns to announce the fact of their children's birth and the names they have given them. Mostly they stick to the tried and true. It is hard for a newcomer to fight its way into the top 10.

Then there is the tell-tale male egotism which decrees that first sons be named after their fathers or, if the unfortunate first born happens to be a girl, she be given a female adaptation of Dad's name. Such was the origin of Roberta, Henrietta, Georgina and, cop this, Nigella. But surely Johnene is taking things a bit far (I've even heard of Johnette), not to mention the latest, which I'm told is Briana.

A British import who once ran one of our arts institutions and was evidently of a classical bent called his children Caractacus and Boadicea. 'Caractacus, stop picking on Boadicea' would play well in the supermarket.

TV soapies have a lot to answer for. Kylies and Jasons have doubtless already flooded the market. A whole sociological theory can probably be constructed on the fact that you are much more likely to hear Tiffany and Troy in Rooty Hill than in Bellevue Hill. A name is the only fancy 'gift' many people can afford to give their children.

30 January 1991

BAH, HUMBUG TO THIS SILLY FEEDING FRENZY

Christians may detect an ironic symmetry in the fact that the Ceausescus met their nemesis on Christmas Day.

It is reported that, at the news of their execution, church bells tolled and the devout applauded the death of the anti-Christ. It was recalled that the public celebration of the religious festival had been banned by the communists on their ascension to power in 1946. Its *de facto* restoration marked the end of a dark age.

No doubt there will be many who will interpret the political earthquake which has devastated communist regimes in

Eastern Europe as the triumph of Christianity over Marxism.

In Poland, the Catholic Church, with a Polish Pope at its head, played a central role in providing moral, and no doubt material, support to Lech Walesa's Solidarity Movement. The surrender of the communists to Solidarity may be said to be the catalyst that set dominoes tumbling throughout Poland's neighbouring countries.

But even if we overlook the simplistic nature of such an explanation of the events of the *Annus Mirabilis* 1989, there could be no greater mistake than to extrapolate from the perceived Christian triumph in Europe a bright future for the institution of Christmas in Australia.

Every year, we are reminded in a jejune editorial in this paper of the meaning of Christmas. The message reads increasingly like a commercial, an attempt to sell something, rather than a description of anything real.

I suggest that Christmas be renamed the Festival of Grace and David. People will get the message without any mention of Brothers or Jones. At least that would acknowledge the reality that Christmas in this country is a shopping spree which has nothing - except for a dwindling minority - to do with religion, unless shopping is to be recognised as the great Australian religion.

It can be argued that the reason Christmas in Eastern Europe has retained more of its religious flavour than here is that there was nothing to buy in the shops there. An economic system which can fill the shelves with goods is obviously a more effective way of taking Christ out of Christmas than its abolition by decree of the State.

Communism aided and abetted the survival of religious fervour by failing to provide substitutes. When European civilisation was exported to Australia in the closing years of the 18th century, the package included several customs which were quite anachronistic in a country with our climate.

One was the habit of judges and barristers loading themselves up in any season with the protective clothing of a polar bear. The encumbrance of wigs and gowns on a muggy

Sydney day remains as an illustration of the conservatism of the law.

Another was the traditional northern hemisphere Christmas, which is essentially a cold-climate thing. Over there, no cruelty was involved in clothing Santa Claus in whiskers and heavy gear, but here it amounts to officially condoned torture.

Over there, it was a natural time for people to want to huddle together in family groups around a fire, gorge themselves on warming food and grog, and to enjoy the spectacles provided in their magnificent churches.

Here, the seasonal ambience is hedonistic and dispersive. It is a time of cricket, tennis, and skin cancer. People want to be out of doors and engaged in mindless pursuits.

It is not a time for reflecting on the mysteries of life or eternal salvation. It is a time of fast foods, rather than laboriously cooked turkeys and plum puddings.

Another factor which has done much to undermine the old-fashioned Christmas is the women's movement. Christmas was the most sexist time of the year.

Not only did women accept the burden of fighting ther way through the crowds in excessive heat to do the shopping (they still do) while their menfolk celebrated with 'the boys', but, on the Big Day itself, it was the women who sweated over the hot stove and kept the ankle-biters in some sort of order, while the men enjoyed a few cleansing ales in the backyard.

There has been no shopping revolt yet but there is a growing female revulsion for the kitchen-sinkery which is inseparable from the old-fashioned Christmas.

Then again, we have an increasing number of citizens to whom Christmas is meaningless. The multicultural society which, despite the Blaineys, Ruxtons, and Caseys, is an irreversible trend in this country, will further dilute the traditional Christmas.

In short, as the communists have taught us, just about the only way to secure the survival of the old-fashioned Christmas is to abolish it. We've had some silly governments but we are unlikely to get one as foolish as that.

Well, 1989 was some year, wasn't it? It not only saw the end of Noriega, the Ceausescus, and an assortment of puffed-up little geriatric Stalins, but also of Leona M. Helmsley.

A few, but not enough, of our own megalomaniacs also bit the dust. There has been a revival of hope among those who, like myself, had begun to believe that justice had deserted this planet.

2 January 1990

DULL CHORES OF THE RICH AND FAMOUS

Book-launching is a growth industry because so many are being published that a book's birth must, if possible, be turned into a public event, which may even be noticed by the media.

My name seems to crop up quite often when people are looking for someone to launch a book.

Being a book-launcher is not as simple as you might think. Usually you have to steel yourself for nearly undrinkable 'launch-wine' but also, if you are at all conscientious, you have to read the book, which is not always pleasurable.

This has been my lucky week. On Monday, I launched a book which is wonderful – and even the wine was OK. The book itself is a beautiful artefact, published by Angus and Robertson.

It is called *The Australian Writers' Book of Days* and it was compiled from the Mitchell Library's extensive collection of original manuscripts by John Murphy, senior manuscripts librarian of the State Library of NSW.

It consists of extracts from the diaries of notable Australians and a few others who have made an impact on our history. For good measure, there are beautifully produced illustrations, photographed with great skill from the original documents from which this book was compiled.

It is comforting for ordinary mortals to discover that the humdrum, the unremarkable, plays as big a role in the lives of famous (or merely well-known) people as in our own. This clearly emerges from their diaries.

Here is the entry of one of our best novelists, Eleanor Dark, written in the Blue Mountains in January 1941: 'Dull, dampish, rather chilly. Chores all morning except for a half-hour writing.' If I kept a diary, you might expect something like that from me, writing in the same Blue Mountains some 50 years on.

Life has changed a lot since Philip Parker King, son of Philip Gidley King, First Fleeter and later Governor of NSW, penned his diary entry in April, 1818.

What has not changed is the subject of his entry: 'The flies here are very numerous and troublesome, literally eating the meat out of our mouths . . .'

A famous man in his day was Sir Walter Baldwin Spencer, biologist, anthropologist, collector and patron of Australian art.

There's a certain drollery in discovering that this man, who was a shade more distinguished than that modern corporate cowboy, John Elliott, shared one of his passions: Sir Walter was president of the Victorian Football League.

Dorothea Mackellar, famous for 'I love a sunburnt country', made this diary entry for 5 April 1911: 'Dad told me that a boy at the Grammar School published *Core of My Heart* as his the other day. Funny.' (Her poem had been published under that name in London in 1908.) Dear Dorothea, in your grave, that sort of thing still goes on after all these years, as Frederick Forsyth can attest.

On a November day in 1842, the architect Edmund Blacket, who was to do so much to beautify the face of Sydney with his elegant churches and other buildings, sailed into Sydney Harbour and recorded his impressions as follows: 'As we sailed up to the Town we passed all the points and coves of this magnificent harbour, and I thought I never saw so exquisite a scene.'

I wonder what he'd think of what his successors in his trade had done to that wonderfully endowed scene. I make bold to suggest his verdict would be closer to that of Neville Gruzman than that of Harry Seidler.

And Lloyd Rees, then aged 21, caught his first glimpse of the harbour, whose glories he was to capture and preserve, whatever outrages the developers might ultimately perpetrate on its foreshores and hinterland, from the deck of the *SS Canberra* on a December day in 1916.

His diary entry for that day records his impression of 'a dream of green, pink and blue' – which he later transferred to canvas.

Havelock Ellis, too, was only a boy of 18 when he settled in Sydney for three years in 1877, 20 years before publishing the work which made him famous, *Studies in the Psychology of Sex*.

But already his mind was on the main game, if I may apply a favourite term of Paul Keating's to something a little more exhilarating than economics.

Young Havelock's diary entry for 1 September 1877, includes these words: 'There is in all of us who possess any sensibility at all . . . a tendency to love, a tendency which will always create some object and will cause it to be loved in some way.'

But the poor lad evidently got off to a bad start because he also records that his fancy 'has chosen one who shows no sign of returning it if it were presented to her'. How could those Sydney girls have known he would one day be world-renowned?

What a pity it is that men and women cannot become beneficiaries of the well-known aphrodisiac quality of fame until after they have earned it, and that it is not available to them when they need it most in their randy adolescence.

In an era of much undeserved celebrity, it is somehow reassuring to be reminded that even genuine celebrities have their dull moments.

28 November 1990

A REPUBLIC? AXE THE STATES FIRST

I wish the newly born Australian Republican Movement good luck. I also applaud the resolution sponsored by John Dawkins at the recent ALP national conference to work for an Australian republic by the year 2001.

But is it really something to get into a lather about? In the first flush of outrage following Sir John Kerr's coup in 1975, I joined notables like Donald Horne, Patrick White and others on platforms where we attempted to promote the republican cause. But as the rage subsided, the steam soon went out of the nascent republican crusade. It obviously struck most people as pretty marginal to their real concerns.

It would, of course, be demeaning if the absurd achronism of our colonial tie with the 'mother country' should see out the century, even in its present attenuated form. But surely it rates a fair way down the scale of necessary changes in the governmental structure of this country. Below, for instance, the abolition of State governments. I suggest to republicans that their reforming fervour would be better employed in persuading the citizenry to shed this superfluous and expensive baggage (while not discounting their campaign for a republic).

One of the reasons why politicians are so much on the nose in Australia is that there are far too many of them. Voters who are obliged (it feels like every year) on pain of being fined to choose between Tweedledum and Tweedledee in State and federal elections, may be excused for questioning whether a country of 17 million people needs nearly 800 professional politicians (not counting local councillors).

The politician-to-population ratio in the main member States of the British Commonwealth has been calculated (Ken

Thomas, *Regional Self Government, A Structure for a Modern Australian Constitition*, 1991) as follows: Australia (787 politicians), 1 to 20 000; New Zealand (95), 1 to 35 000; Canada (386), 1 to 66 000; United Kingdom (650), 1 to 145 000. Tasmania is a world leader with one full-time politician per 6611 people! The ultimate in over-government was reached a few years ago with the setting up of a local 'parliament' for the ACT, against the specific wishes of the natives.

Why do we hear almost nothing about the incubus of State governments from the vociferous advocates of 'leaner' government? In this situation, conducting a ten-year campaign just to get rid of the royal tie seems something like advocating the amputation of a little toe to cure a gangrenous foot.

The apathy towards the curse of over-government is probably to be explained by what is seen as the near impossibility of achieving such a drastic change. Scepticism is supported by the failure of most referendums to alter the constitution even in comparatively minor respects.

But how did we achieve federation in the first place? In the middle years of last century, people with some political vision could perceive the roadblock to national progress implicit in a system of unfederated colonies, bedevilled by tariff brawls and provincial self-interest. They must have experienced a similar feeling of despair about the prospects of ever changing our constitutional arrangements.

As early as 1847, Earl Grey, the Secretary of State for the Colonies, proposed that a 'central authority' be created in Australia to regulate matters affecting more than one colony. This caused alarm in some of the colonies which feared domination by NSW, and nothing came of it. There were some desultory federal initiatives in the 1850s, notably from William Wentworth. But in the period between 1860 and 1880, federation was seldom mentioned.

However, the efforts of powerful, energetic figures like Sir Henry Parkes, Sir Samuel Griffith and Alfred Deakin, began to bear fruit, and on 1 March 1891, 45 delegates assembled in Sydney for the first sessions of the National Australasian

Convention. Although a draft constitution emerged from that elite gathering, the great depression of the 1890s soon absorbed all of the country's political and economic energies, and federation was again off the agenda.

But the question was too urgent to be dismissed forever and the Federal Conventions of 1897–1898 led to the referendum campaigns of 1898–1900. These campaigns culminated in the birth of the Commonwealth of Australia on 1 January 1901.

The faint hearts of that period have their counterparts today, who dismiss the possibility of eliminating State governments as a pipedream. But we live in an era when ideas and institutions which were thought to be set in stone are being discarded daily.

The duplication of functions and bureaucracies inherent in our present system, not to mention the dangerous disrepute into which government itself is falling because of the superfluity of posturing politicians, must surely be obvious to economic rationalists who are today in the ascendant.

A system of government comprising a president, a single-chamber federal parliament and a series of regional authorities with well-defined powers and functions could cut the number of politicians at least by half and eliminate thousands of paper-shufflers from the public payroll.

Of course it will be hard to achieve, as was federation. That is why I would prefer to see our best minds devoted to the task of selling the public the need for a drastic modernisation of our horse-and-buggy system of government rather than concentrating their energies on one small detail which is of not much more than symbolic significance.

17 July 1991

FATHOMING THE MAGIC OF A GENIUS

The Patrick White I knew for nearly thirty years was a fierce and fearsome moralist, bountifully generous and sometimes mean-spirited, sage about human weakness and waspishly intolerant, sophisticated and naive, lovable and unbearable.

In short, a human being, but in his case all his virtues and foibles were multiplied by his genius.

Such was the spell he cast that he could always count on a handful of acolytes prepared to grant him an exemption from the usual norms of civility.

My feeling towards him fluctuated between affection, reverence and exasperation. Looking back on the vicissitudes of our relationship, I turned up my copy of his last novel, *Memoirs of Many In One*. It is inscribed to me in his spidery handwriting in terms which for him were adulatory.

But, as I once told him, it was a short step from his pantheon to his doghouse.

Soon after that encomium I was in disfavour. My offence? My wife and I had accepted an invitation from Sir Ninian and Lady Stephen to dine at Yarralumla.

One of the crusades Patrick and I shared was republicanism, the need for Australia to sever the tie with royalty, the final burial of the cringe to mother Britain. After Sir John Kerr had pulled the rug from beneath the Whitlam government, Patrick and I spoke from the same platform on this subject.

Whatever may be said about the difficulties of his prose style, his speeches were models of simple eloquence.

When, some 10 years after 11 November 1975, my wife and I received our invitation from the Stephens, we accepted, on the principle that the office (of which we still disapproved) could be distinguished from its occupants, whom we liked and respected.

To Patrick, for whom the daily Vice Regal column was obligatory reading (to keep his hit list up to date), this amounted to apostasy.

His moral inflexibility, which was his great strength, was also his greatest weakness. But the brownie points I had accumulated soon earned me forgiveness and I think, at the end I rated, if not in his pantheon, at least not in his by then overpopulated doghouse.

Patrick rarely talked about himself. Thus I was rather taken aback when he said to me out of the blue one day a couple of years ago: 'My insights came from my homosexuality.' He pronounced the first 'o' as in not.

He never mentioned his novels and seemed somewhat put out when others did.

Shortly after the publication of *Riders in the Chariot*, a Jewish friend of mine asked him at a dinner party at my house: 'Is Himmelfarb (a Jewish character in the novel) based on anybody in particular?' Patrick answered coldly: 'He is mostly imagined.'

On another occasion as he entered my house, I inquired: 'How do you like my Godfrey Miller?', pointing to a painting by that artist I had recently acquired. He threw the picture a quick, almost hostile glance and said tersely: 'I think I've got Godfrey Miller out of my system.'

This was shortly after the publication of *The Vivisector*. I had formed a tentative opinion, from certain clues in the book that the central character, Hurtle Duffield, owed something to Godfrey Miller, but I would never have dared to ask Patrick if this was so. I felt quite triumphant at what I took to be an oblique confirmation of my hunch.

Only once did I know him to admit that one of his characters was drawn from life.

He told me a hilarious anecdote about a particularly odious character he had met, with that deep chuckle which garnished his malice, concluding with: 'I got square with him. I put him into one of my books.'

The work which he considered the most satisfying of his output was *The Twyborn Affair*.

While he was writing it he rang me from time to time to check on some minor matter of legal mores on which he thought I might be knowledgeable, such as whether lawyers' womenfolk were permitted to attend tribal gatherings, for example bench-and-bar dinners.

Although his fiction was at the furthest possible remove from social realism, he was a stickler for accuracy of detail.

His generosity, which he did his best to conceal, was unbounded. Jack Mundey, whom Patrick rightly admired, told me he once asked him for a donation to some cause, hoping for perhaps $200. Patrick gave him $5000.

When the Nimrod Theatre went out of business in Belvoir Street, Surry Hills, and the building was about to be demolished, Patrick was a major subscriber to the new company set up to keep the place going as a theatre, which is still thriving.

He was a formidable hater. This was because he reposed in people who attracted his admiration hopes which very few of them could fulfil. When he finally detected their imperfections his extravagant expectations of them turned to equally extravagant loathing.

His demanding moral standards imposed a strain on his relationships and magnified the disappointments life deals out to all of us.

He was a noble man, perhaps just a little too much so.

10 October 1990

WHITE: MOVING, PROFOUND AND DUTIFUL

Patrick White Speaks
by Patrick White
Primavera Press

Speaking from a Town Hall balcony facing Sydney Square on 11 November 1976, the first anniversary of Kerr's sacking of the Whitlam Government, Patrick White declared: 'The days of saying, "Oh, I'm not political – I couldn't care less – I vote informal" – one would like to think that sort of thing is past.'

I was with him that day on the balcony. We who would once never have dared to ask him to tear himself away from his creative desk to espouse some public cause had come to realise that, on a selected list of issues, he was prepared to mount the rostrum. He never liked doing it but he had come to regard it as a painful duty. The list included environmental issues, nuclear disarmament, uranium mining, republicanism, the monorail and the bicentennial celebrations, which he regarded as an obscenity.

This timely book published by Primavera Press is a collection of Patrick White's public speeches beginning in 1972 at a family picnic rally in his beloved Centennial Park to protest against a proposal by the NSW Government to take over sections of the park for an Olympic sports complex, and culminating in a speech to the students of La Trobe University in 1988.

The prevailing tone is moral outrage at humanity's desecration of the planet, contempt for almost all of our posturing politicians for ignoring or lying about the most important problems and an almost nightmarish awareness of the nuclear threat hanging over us.

Politicians, who consider themselves experts in invective, may derive some lessons from this book in how to excoriate a foe without descending into the sewer. If you have a wit and a vocabulary like White's, you don't have to resort to 'sleazebags' or jargon or Hawkespeak.

Here are some random samples. Dealing with gaps in the Constitution which had made possible the perversion of democracy in 1975, he remarks, 'but when the maggots begin to appear on the meat, you have to look at the fly-proof safe'.

Our Prime Minister is not one of his favourite characters, as indicated by his reference to 'Hawkie, screaming from under his cockatoo hairdo the platitudes he has got by heart'.

He refers to Bond, 'who hovers over the corpse of democratic Chile like an obscene Blowie', and to Reagan as 'a figure from one of his own B-films'.

But these are merely side-swipes. White is deadly serious about the matters on which he chooses to speak publicly. There is much that is both moving and profound in these pieces. Though always regarded as a reclusive man he throws considerable light on the sources of his own inspiration and on the forces which drew him back irresistibly from an expatriate life.

Speaking at Grenfell, Henry Lawson's birthplace, at a festival in honour of the poet in 1984, he referred to Lawson's attempts to escape what he regarded as 'the grey monotony of Australian life' and he made this comment: 'Henry, like many others, found that he could not escape. He was driven back, I suspect, as I was by glimmers of remembered landscape, by scents and sounds from hot days – drawn, not necessarily "back to the womb" to quote the frequent accusation, but to childhood, the source of creation, when perception is at its sharpest.'

In another place he says: 'The essence of what you have to say you pick up before you're 20 . . .'

For me the most moving piece is the last in the book, his

1988 speech at La Trobe University, in which he spoke of 'moral distinction' and used Ben Chifley as an exemplar. He also invented the word 'kidults' to describe that large proportion of grown Australians who remain children at heart. And he delivered his verdict on his fellows: 'I believe most people hunger after spirituality, even if that hunger remains in many cases unconscious.'

It is a joy to read taut, uncluttered prose with nary a cliché, shaped by a steadfast eschewal of the mawkish and the modish.

For good measure there are a hitherto unpublished sardonic poem and a few photographs of Patrick smiling benignly – at his dog and his cat.

20 August 1989

EVERY HOST DESERVES A ROMEO

'Good night, good night. Parting is such sweet sorrow, that I shall say good night till it be morrow.'

So spake Romeo and promptly shot through like a Bondi tram. I have often had occasion to wish that his attitude to departure was more universally followed. I have always considered myself a reasonably gregarious man and I recall with joy the many convivial lunches and dinners in which I have participated, garnished with good, encouragingly lubricated conversation.

But I have always believed that there comes a time when people, both hosts and guests, have had enough of each other for the time being. In short, it's time to go.

Having reached that decision, I am ready to do a Romeo. But, in my experience, social disengagement is mostly not so much an act as a process, not a sweet sorrow but a prolongation of an occasion which has already petered out.

Instead of the curtain falling it gets stuck halfway down with the characters lolling around, not knowing how to bring the play to a close.

Although I am not game to do it myself, I believe it should be socially acceptable on such occasions for the host to do the equivalent of putting the chairs up on the table or of the pub chucker-out calling: 'Time, gentlemen, please.'

It's a subject on which the Bride and I have agreed to differ. To put it more bluntly, I have been overruled. She tells me that it is impolite to leave abruptly. I do not suggest that she is being unduly idiosyncratic in taking this attitude. In fact, it appears that her view of parting is the norm and it is mine that is aberrant.

Sometimes, I suspect that it is the ageing process which affects my view that it is time for a social sergeant-major to proclaim: 'Company! Dismiss.' But that cannot be true since I was of this opinion long before entering the sere and yellow.

So, there I sit or stand pinned to the wall by a friend whom I may greatly esteem but who has reached, as we all tend to do, the repetitious stage.

To many people the process of parting appears to be the most enjoyable part of the occasion. They wish to prolong it as much as possible.

Standing interminably in doorways or on the path between door and gate seems to such folk to provide the real spice of social intercourse. (Is it because this is when the most indiscreet confidences slip out?)

I have been assured by a much travelled friend that this habit is peculiarly Australian. She tells me that in the most polite circles in London or New York nobody bats an eyelid when, at a certain stage, guests look at their watches, announce they are leaving – and leave.

The Bard had the first word and he shall have the last. As Macbeth put it:

'If it were done, when 'tis done, then 'twere well it were done quickly.'

I have never regarded these as Shakespeare's pithiest lines

but I welcome his support for the proposition I am advancing.

When I put this to the Bride, she protested that Macbeth was talking about an assassination he had in mind, not the termination of a lunch or a dinner party. I concede there's a difference, but I'll bet a few hosts and hostesses have sometimes felt an urge towards assassination. I certainly have.

PENGUIN - THE BEST AUSTRALIAN READING

Waiting for the Revolution Noel McLachlan

What, if anything, is distinctive about being Australian? When and how did our nationalism begin? Did the convicts have anything to do with it? What about Eureka, Ned Kelly, the *Bulletin* and the Heidelberg painters? These issues are explored as we near the beginning of the 21st century.

Furious Agreement Michael Dugan

To celebrate the fiftieth year of its founding the Australian Institute of Management invited forty Australians distinguished in the fields of business, the arts and humanities, politics and the sciences to consider what they saw as the vital issues for our future over the next fifty years. The result is a provocative and stimulating collection of essays notable as much for its differences of opinion as its furious agreement about the need for change.

PENGUIN – THE BEST AUSTRALIAN READING

PENGUIN - THE BEST AUSTRALIAN READING

The Penguin Book of Australian Verse
Edited with an Introduction by Harry Heseltine

In this widely acclaimed anthology, Professor Harry Heseltine has collected Australian poetry from every major period, covering the work of more than one hundred of Australia's leading poets – from Charles Harpur, Henry Kendall and Adam Lindsay Gordon to Les Murray, Geoffrey Lehmann and Michael Dransfield.

In addition to providing brief biographies of each poet, the editor has contributed an introduction to the book, in which he discusses his choice of material and provides a scholarly review of Australian poetry.

The Penguin Book of Modern Australian Poetry
Edited by John Tranter and Philip Mead

This book answers the need for a widely representative and credible anthology of modern Australian poetry, as seen from the last decade of the twentieth century. Beginning with Kenneth Slessor, it offers a challenging view of 'early modern' Australian poetry up until the 1960s. It also presents the decade of turmoil from 1965 to 1975 in a new light, identifying currents of energy among the younger writers, and balancing new reputations with old. And it reveals the twenty-five years from 1965 through to the 1990s as a time of growing vigour and diversity.

PENGUIN – THE BEST AUSTRALIAN READING

The State of Play Leonard Radic

The last thirty years have seen the development of a vigorous Australian theatre, addressing issues of importance in our national life. The movement began in the late 1960s in both Sydney and Melbourne where young writers, actors and directors, most of them fresh out of university, looked at the mostly imported theatre of the day and decided that it was stuffy, outmoded and irrelevant, and that a new home-grown drama was needed. The result was La Mama and the Pram Factory in Melbourne and the Nimrod in Sydney: companies which in a few short years did much to revolutionise the Australian theatre scene, as well as producing important new writers whose names have become household words, among them Jack Hibberd, David Williamson, John Romeril and Alex Buzo.

Leonard Radic, a playwright himself, has reviewed more than 2000 productions for the *Age*. In *The State of Play* he draws on his long experience and on interviews with playwrights and directors to create a lively picture of the emergence and subsequent development of a truly Australian theatre.